How God Became Man

A DIVINE MYSTERY

Expose' of the Virgin Mary and the Incarnation of Christ

New Revelations

ENEL MALAKRIST

Copyright 2022 by Enel Malakrist

ISBN: 978-0-9884558-8-7

All rights reserved. No part of this book may be used or reproduced in any manner whatsoever, without written permission, except in the case of brief quotations embodied in critical articles or reviews, and religious teachings.

Unless otherwise indicated, the Bible quotations are taken from the King James Version of the Bible. Copyright 1945 by Oxford University Press inc.

Statement of Purpose

This book is inspired by a dream, in which the Lord said to the author, "My people need teaching. Go!" The purpose of this book is to dispel false beliefs relating to the conception of the Virgin Mary, and the Incarnation of Christ, and to reveal through Scriptures, the mystery of how the invisible God crossed over from the eternal realm and appeared in the material world in the form of a man.

Table of Contents

Statement of Purpose... iii

Chapter 1: How God made Man..1

Chapter 2: The Fall of Man...8

Chapter 3: The Seed of the Woman 14

Chapter 4: Angelic Annunciations...18

Chapter 5: In the Fullness of Time 23

Chapter 6: Intervening Politics..26

Chapter 7: Quirinius...32

Chapter 8: More Evidences 38

Chapter 9: Preview of the Nativity 40

Chapter 10: The Night When Jesus Was Born....................................43

Chapter 11: Bethlehem Shepherds 46

Chapter 12: The Wise Men..49

Chapter 13: What is Christmas?..58

Chapter 14: Concept of Incarnation..61

Chapter 15: Doctrine of the Incarnation of Christ 63

Chapter 16: Religious Malpractice 67

Chapter 17: The Catholic Hypothesis 71

Chapter 18: Never in the Womb 74

Chapter 19: How God Became Man 77

Chapter 20: False Doctrines 83

Chapter 21: A Message to the Churches 89

Chapter 22: A Vision of Hell...94

References 100

Chapter 1
How God made Man

America was founded on Christian principles, and the Holy Bible was the nation's guidebook. Two hundred and forty years later, America has evolved into a nation in which the majority of her people reject God. A recent Gallop Poll suggests that a mere forty percent of Americans now believe that God created the universe and man.

A recent scientific article highlights the trending atheistic views. In that article, astrophysicists claim that planetary intelligence exists. The learned men implied that the universe evolved on its own and acquired a collective body of knowledge in the process.

The astrophysicists further hypothesized that the planets then applied that knowledge across the universe in a harmonious way that benefits the entire system. It's like saying that the chess pieces are intelligent, and they make their own moves and as thus are not merely created objects.

The scientists should realize that dumb objects can only perform in the manner that they were programmed. The chess pieces cannot move at all without an intelligent master. Likewise, the planets move only at the will of their creator and supernatural master. Therefore, whether Americans or astrophysicists believe it or not, the truth stands; God is the irrefutable creator of the universe and of man. Moreover, it is God who controls the universe and harmonizes the movements of the stars and planets.

Primeval Civilization

In the dateless past, God created the heavens and the earth. The Bible says that God created the great lights, Genesis 1:16. God stretches out the heavens, controls the sun and the stars, and performs wonders that cannot be fathomed. See Job 9: 7-8

The universe was not created by mechanical means. Neither was it formed from any pre-existing materials. The Bible reveals that the Almighty God spoke the universe into existence. He called the stars and planets into being. The omniscient God created time and space. God created all things visible and invisible. See Psalm 33:6, Hebrews 11:3. God created the universe out of nothing. All things appeared instantly at his command; and not over millions of years by evolution as scientists hypothesize.

However, the Scriptures indicate that Earth was not created in the beginning. Neither was it created by the word of God. The Bible reveals that God made the Earth with his hand. And when it was completed: "The morning stars sang together, and the sons of God (Angels) shouted for joy".[1] This clearly shows that the stars were created before the Earth was formed.

Scriptures reveal that God did not create Earth to be an empty void. Earth was the crown jewel of the material worlds. God created it to be inhabited by living creatures.[2] He made it habitable by natural beings. He provided an abundant supply of water, life-supporting gasses, food, and everything that living creatures need to survive.

Earth's First Sinful Civilization

God created numerous species of animals, plants, fish. He also made man on Earth. God declared "I have made the Earth and created man upon it".[3] The first social system on Earth existed thousands of years before Adam was created.

However, the primeval civilization rebelled against God.[4] They rejected godly laws and established a godless, lawless and violent society.

God was displeased with those people. There was no hope of recovery, or sanity to the nations. There was no remedy. Consequently, divine judgment was determined against the primeval nations, and the destruction of Earth was decreed.

Divine Wrath

The planet was devastated by a great catastrophe, which completely altered its surface. Many large meteors travelling at tremendous speeds bombarded the earth. Massive amounts of dust rose from those impacts. The dust formed dark clouds above the earth. Very large craters marking the points of meteoric impacts are located in North America, Europe and Asia.

Scientists believe the Barringer crater in Arizona was caused by a large meteor crashing on the earth. They believe that the event occurred about fifty thousand years ago. There was also the Chicxulub crater in the Yucatan Peninsula. This is believed to be caused by a very large meteor. Scientists suggest that this meteor impact caused the extinction of the dinosaurs.

Earth's punishment continued with many powerful volcanic eruptions all over the world. The ash from the eruptions rose high above the earth. This together with the dust from the meteor impacts, formed a thick impenetrable barrier in the stratosphere. This barrier blocked sunlight and heat from reaching the earth. No sunlight could penetrate the dark clouds and the mist, and all living things on Earth perished.

Powerful earthquakes also shook the earth. Devastating tsunamis ensued and water from the oceans rushed inland and covered the mountains.[5] The planet became extremely cold. Consequently, water on the Earth froze, and the planet became a huge block of ice. That devastating weather condition initiated the great ice age with the Earth becoming a cold, dark, dead and desolate planet.

This primeval flood must not be confused with Noah's flood. The mechanics of the catastrophes were totally different. The Bible says that the waters of the Primeval floods came from the deep (oceans) and covered the land. Then at the time of restoration, God commanded, and they hasted away. The water rushed back to the ocean basins in one day.[6] Not so with Noah's floods. The Scriptures reveal that the waters of Noah's floods were caused by rain. The rain fell continuously for forty days and nights. See Genesis 7:4. Then the flood abated after one hundred and fifty days, and receded steadily for months before the Earth became dry.[7]

A New Epoch

After Earth served its ordained time of punishment, God came down to the cold, flooded, dark and desolate planet. He put an end to the ice-age, and repaired, and restored Earth to its original beauty and purpose. God's first act was to remove the water from the land-mass. The Bible says that Spirit of God moved above the waters, and they rushed back to fill the ocean basins from which they came.[8]

Next, God removed the curse of darkness that shrouded the earth. That act allowed light and heat to reach its surface. Next, God restored the air, the land and the surface waters. God then created vegetation, new species of plants, animals, fish, birds, and all living creatures. Some are large, and some small and some invisible. God fully restored the ecology, and the beauty of Earth. He then decreed a sustainable recycling system of life preserving gasses and water, and harmonized the biosphere.

Venerable Man

God then introduced a second social system on planet earth. God purposed to make man in his own image and likeness. And so, God's final act of restoration of the Earth was to create man. The Bible says that, "The LORD God formed man out of the dust of the ground". Scriptures reveal that God used clay to form the body of the first man. All the body parts were completed along with the internal organs. The first man had eyes but could not see, ears but could not hear, and lungs but could not breathe. He was just a lifeless body lying on the ground. The body was perfectly made, but it was not functional because man was not yet made complete.

Then God created the human spirit and "breathed into his nostrils the breath of life; and man became a living soul."[9] Adam's lungs expanded as he received his first breath, and he came to life. All his organs began to function, and Adam became conscious of his surroundings.

Observe that the creation of man was a two-step process. Firstly, God formed the physical and physiological, parts of man from materials that were already created. Notice that the spirit was not created at the same time as the body. So, the body was first made ready, and then God created the psychological part of man. God created the human spirit and infuses it into him. The complete man is therefore, a combination of a physical nature and a spirit nature.

The first man was named Adam. The name Adam in Hebrew means, 'son of the red earth'. This suggests that God formed the first man out of red clay. For a short period of time, Adam was the only human being on the earth. He was very lonely, and God made a female companion for him.

God put Adam into a deep sleep and removed flesh from his body, and made a woman. Adam named her Eve. God also created a human spirit and infused it into Eve. God then blessed the couple as man and wife.

Observe that the spirit gave Adam life. Therefore, the body without the spirit is dead. The Bible also declares that God creates and owns all human spirits. The Scriptures states that at death the spirit leaves the body and returns to God who gave it.[10]

Procreation Ordered

Adam was created first then Eve. After Adam and Eve were created, God declared the law of procreation. That law was the divine command whereby man would propagate the Earth with human species.

God said to the man and the woman, "Be fruitful and multiply."[11] He told them to go and produce children and people have been doing that since creation. Adam is therefore acknowledged as the progenitor of the human race.

God then made it easy and pleasant for the man and the woman to reproduce, and have children. God equipped them with the tools to do the job. He equipped the man with the organs to produce male gamete, and the woman with organs to produce the egg.

The male gamete fertilizes the egg inside the womb. The microscopic cells unite to form one unit when the woman conceives, and biological life begins. The cells divide multiple times forming an embryo. The embryo grows rapidly and become encased in a sack containing water, called amniotic fluid. The sack is in the uterus (womb) and is connected to the placenta by the umbilical cord. The placenta in turn is attached to the walls of the woman's uterus.

The embryo grows and begins to take the shape of a person. At that point the embryo is called a fetus. The fetus is submerged in a sack containing amniotic fluid. It develops eyes, lips, nose, and lungs, and all the internal organs. All the organs with opening to the outside are sealed shut to prevent the fetus from drowning. Likewise, the lungs remain in a collapsed state.

The fetus is totally dependent upon the host (mother), and is kept alive and nutritionally sustained by the mother. The fetus moves freely in the sack containing amniotic fluid. However, its movements are involuntary, and it subconsciously reacts to outside stimulus.

Because the fetus is attached to the mother by the placenta, and the umbilical cord, it is therefore not an individual person. The attachment makes the fetus a part of the mother's physical structure.

Moreover, the fetus is totally dependent upon the mother for its survival. The fetus is not a person, because a person cannot live inside another person. Since the fetus is not a person, it has no individual rights or civil rights, or human rights. It's rights are invested in the mother's rights, for nine months or for as long it is in the womb. However, the status of the fetus changes at birth when it becomes a person.

Observe that procreation follows the same pattern of the creative principle laid down by God in the beginning. That pattern follows throughout all generations. Man participates in the forming of the body by producing the male gamete, and the woman by producing the egg. The woman also sustains the fetus as it develops in her womb.

The human part in procreation is limited to producing the physical body of the person. But the physical body is not the whole man as demonstrated in the act of the creation of man.

God also plays the key role in procreation. Man is made up of a body, a soul and a spirit. The spirit is of a higher nature, and cannot not be formed in the womb. However, immediately as the fetus separates from the mother, God creates the human spirit, and gives it to the baby with its first breath. All humans are therefore created individually, and each is unique with a mind of his own.

Gestation

In a normal pregnancy, the fetus matures within nine months after which the baby is now ready to be delivered. The placenta separates from the uterus and the fetus departs from the womb. The fetus is now deprived of oxygen as a result of the disconnected placenta.

Moreover, during the birth process the fetus lungs remain collapsed. The fetal air passages are blocked, and it cannot breathe. It is therefore literally dead for a short period of time during the birth process. The limp body comes out and the nostrils becomes unblocked. Instantly, God creates and infuses the human spirit into it, and gives it life. The baby then takes his first breath, and cries.

The divine infusion of the human spirit in the baby completes the process of procreation. The new born baby now becomes a human being. He now possesses all the rights and privileges of a person.

Observe the pattern of God's creative act. He gives the human spirit to the child at birth. Just as it was in the beginning. Thereby the new-born baby receives a physical nature and a spiritual nature, and both co-exist in every living human being.

Chapter 2

The Fall of Man

In the beginning, man sinned by transgressing the word of God. Man knew from the beginning that the penalty for sin is death. God laid down that law after man was created. The Scriptures declare that the soul that sinneth shall die. As a consequence, man was divinely placed under the penalty of death. There are three degrees of death. Namely, spiritual death, physical death, and eternal death in that order.

Death causes a separation. Spiritual death is the separation from God due to sin. Adam suffered spiritual death from the moment he transgressed the law of God, and ate the forbidden fruit. He lost fellowship with God and distanced himself from God.

Physical death occurs when a person stops breathing, and the brain no longer functions. At death, the spirit/soul leaves the body. The Scriptures affirm the truth that the body without the spirit is dead. See James 2:26.

Eternal death also involves the spirit/soul. The spirit is created by God in his own image and likeness. The human spirit is therefore indestructible. The human spirit cannot die. Eternal death is like spiritual death in that it causes a separation from God.

However, the two differ in that a person has hope of redemption from spiritual death, but none under eternal death. Eternal death is absolute and irreversible everlasting separation from God. This is final and irreversible punishment for the unrepentant sinners who die in their sins. See Revelation 21:8.

Mankind is under the penalty of death, is lost, and cannot not save himself. Moreover, the Scriptures declare death on all sinners. Man is doomed to suffer death because Adam's sin is passed on to all generations. The apostle Paul wrote saying: "Wherefore, as by one man sin entered into the world; and death by sin; so, death passed upon to all men for that all have sinned."[12]

A Divine Promise

Adam's failure did not surprise the Creator. The Lord God is omniscient. He knows all things past, present and things to come. Scriptures state that God knows the end or the outcome of all things from the beginning. The prophet Isaiah under the anointing of the Spirit wrote these words of the Lord: "I am God, and there is none like me, declaring the end from the beginning, and from ancient times the things that are not yet done, saying, My counsel shall stand, and I will do all my pleasure."[13]

Therefore, God who possesses all wisdom and knowledge, knew, even before he restored the Earth that Adam would fail. However, God by his grace and mercy had a plan to redeem fallen man even before Adam was created.

Nonetheless, there was no free passage for the transgressor of God's law. Divine justice demands the penalty of death for the soul that commits sin. God's justice demands sacrifice for sin. Man is contaminated with sin, and a sinner could not be sacrificed to pay the price of redemption. Man was therefore doomed to die eternally. A sinless man must be found to sacrifice his life to satisfy God's justice. God knew that there would be no one in Adam's race who could qualify as a redeemer.

On that fateful day in the Garden of Eden, God handed down punishments to Adam and Eve for their disobedience. He also rebuked the Devil for causing Adam to sin, and revealed his plan for the redemption of man.

The Redeemer

The main qualification of the Redeemer is that he must be completely free from all sin. This includes inherited sin from Adam. Since sin is perpetuated in the Adam genes, the Redeemer must be free of all the genetic traits of Adam. The Redeemer's blood must be pure and undefiled, and without sin. Therefore, it must be of a higher value than human blood, in order to cover the price of redemption.

Satan defeated man in the Garden of Eden, and God made a promise that the seed (offspring) of the woman would once more battle with Devil, and crush his head. The Devil won the first contest with Adam. Natural man was no match for the angel who has superior powers. However, God promised to even the score. He declared that the seed of the woman would defeat Satan. The seed would restore and redeem man to his original place of fellowship with God.

To accomplish the task, the redeemer must have a greater power than the devil so as to withstand his temptations. The redeemer must be a man and possess the human nature. He must be without sin or blemish. He must be perfect in all his ways.

The seed of the woman must therefore have no trace of Adam's genes. The reason being that Adam's sin passes down to all mankind through his bloodline.

Sin devalues man's blood, so the blood of the redeemer must be of a higher value to pay the price of redemption. The Bible makes it plain that divine justice demands that the soul that sinneth shall die. However, through God's grace and mercy the condemned soul can be redeemed. The divinely ordered price of redemption was atonement through blood.

All men sin at some point in their lives. Therefore, the Lord made provision in the Law that an innocent animal could shed his blood, and

The Fall of Man

die so that the guilty person could live. That innocent victim was always an animal, because animals are not under the curse of Adam's sin.

The principle of the innocent dying for the guilty was first documented in the book of Genesis. The Bible records that God covered the guilty sinners, Adam and Eve, with the skin of an animal. This means that an innocent animal's blood was shed so that they could live, and appear in the presence of God.

Millenniums later animal sacrifice was made a part of the Israel's religious laws. The laws were given to Israel at Mount Horeb in Arabia, as they journeyed through the wilderness. The Scriptures makes it plain that it's the blood that makes atonement. The LORD said to Israel, "For the life of the flesh is in the blood: and I have given it to you upon the altar to make an atonement for your souls: for it is the blood that makes an atonement for the soul."[14]

In reality, animal sacrifice was only a temporary fix because the blood of animals could not atone for sin. Nonetheless, God approved of it so that the children of Israel could appear in His presence.

The reason why animal sacrifices could not atone for sin lies in the value of the blood. An animal is of a lower order than man, and therefore the blood of an animal is of a lower value than that of man. God's justice demands equity, and the animal's blood comes up short, and thus cannot pay the price of redemption.

A man's blood is required to pay for the redemption of man, but man's blood is contaminated with sin. Unfortunately, a sinner cannot redeem a sinner. Angels are of a higher order than man, but they cannot qualify to be a redeemer. Satan had overpowered many angels and caused them to sin and an angel may not be able to defeat him.

Moreover, angels are spirit beings without physical bodies but the redeemer must possess a body to be sacrificed. The body must be capable of suffering death so as to satisfy divine justice.

Divine justice demands death as the price for sin. Angels are spirit beings and cannot die. For that reason, angels cannot redeem man. There was no created being to be found that was qualified to redeem man from the curse of sin.

God's Plan of Redemption

Under the ancient Jewish religious system, God allowed a substitute to die in place of the sinner. To that end, animals were sacrificed for the sin of man. Thousands of animals were slaughtered every year to atone for sin. Those sacrifices did not adequately cover the price for sin, because the life of the animal was valued less that the life of man.

However, the sacrificial system was only a temporary, stop-gap measure. It was established under the Law until a perfect, sinless man could be found. No one on Earth could be found to redeem man. However, God had a plan for the salvation of man. The Scriptures indicate that the plan of redemption was tabled in the Courts of Heaven before God created man.

David under the anointing of the Spirit gave a glimpse of the heavenly discourse. The Psalmist David wrote concerning God's view of animal sacrifice: "Sacrifice and offering thou didst no desire; mine ears hast thou opened: burnt-offering and sin-offering hast thou not required. Then said I: Lo, I come: in the volume of the book, it is written of me. I delight to do thy will, O my God: yea, thy law is written in my heart."[15]

The writer of Hebrews beautifully explained the Psalmist's prophecy. He showed that the only person that was capable of redeeming man was the Creator of all things. God is a Spirit with no form or shape. Yet the Almighty God, the Creator and Ruler of the universe, was willing to set aside His majesty and power, and glory, and appear in human form to redeem sinful mankind.

The writer of Hebrews understood that the animal sacrifice under the Mosaic Law was only a temporary fix for the sin problem. Because the blood of bulls and goats is powerless to erase sins. He observed the Scriptures and discovered that God provided the perfect lamb to be the last acceptable sacrifice for sin. That perfect lamb was Jesus of Nazareth.

The writer of the letter to the Hebrews wrote concerning the divinely appointed Lamb of God that takes away the sin of the world,[16]

"Hence, when Christ entered into the world He said, Sacrifice and offerings You (God) have not desired, but instead you have made ready a body for Me to offer. In burnt offering and sin offerings You (God) have taken no delight. Then said I, Lo, here I am come to do your will, O God; to fulfill what is written of Me (Christ) in the volume of the book."[17]

Chapter 3

The Seed of the Woman

Even though man failed to obey God's divine laws, God did not give up on him, or cast him aside. God was not willing that man should perish. He knew, even before he created Adam, that man would fail so he made a plan to redeem him.

In the beginning, after man sinned, God made provision to restore fellowship with his fallen creatures. God allowed the sacrifice of innocent animals as a substitute for the sinner. Even though the blood of animals could not atone for sin, the merciful and just God accepted the animal sacrifice until a perfect man was found. A man whose blood was equal to, or higher than the value of the blood of Adam's descendants.

No one on Earth could be found because all have sinned. Therefore, God planned to make a way to come into the material world to redeem fallen man from eternal damnation.

The LORD God made a solemn promise in the Garden of Eden that the seed of the woman will overpower and defeat Satan and redeem man.[18] Centuries later, God revealed the nationality of the Seed, and identified him as a Prophet.

As Israel prepared to enter the Promised land, God revealed to Moses that he would send a Prophet who would be born an Israelite. God told Moses that the words of the Prophet would be God's words. Therefore, the people must listen and obey the Prophet or they would be called into judgment.[19]

Centuries passed, and the divinely appointed time came, when God revealed the true identity of the promised seed.

The mystery of how God revealed himself in the flesh is made plain in his creative work. More precisely so, in the creation of man. Accordingly, God created man in His own image and likeness. The human spirit is the part of man that is in the image and likeness of God.

God's plan was to appear in the material world in the form of a man. But God is a Spirit and has no form or shape. God is immortal and invisible. The invisible Spirit of God cannot become flesh. The Scriptures declare that flesh is flesh, and spirit is spirit, and the two natures cannot amalgamate together to form one complex and inseparable unit.

With redemption in mind, God created a place in the physical body of man to house a spirit. Thereby, God made provision for the spirit nature and the flesh nature to unite in one body without fusion. He therefore created a place in man so that the Spirit of God could manifest Himself in human form. Of a surety, the Sovereign God and Creator had the Incarnation of Christ in His divine plan, when He created man in His own image and likeness.

Way of the Seed

A modified process of procreation was the desired means by which the promised seed would be introduced into the world. In the modified form, the source of the divine seed would be from God, and not from humans. Procreation requires an egg and a male gamete (seed). The woman produces the egg, and the man produces the seed.

The seed of Adam came from the Earth because man was created from the dust of the Earth. The seed bearing the genes of Adam was contaminated with sin. Consequently, Adam's seed was rejected for the conception of Mary, because the redeemer must be free of all stain of sin.

As an offspring of Adam, Mary carried his genes in her egg, therefore her egg was contaminated with original sin. Consequently, the

Virgin Mary egg was rejected for the divinely ordained conception. Human reproductive cells were not the basis of the Virgin's conception. The biblical truth is that Mary made no biological contribution to her conception.

The Promised Seed must be pure and holy and without any contamination of sin. The purpose of the Seed was to form a holy tabernacle – a physical body for God. Nothing was found suitable, and God created a new Seed. The angel Gabriel called the seed "holy thing". The seed, or "holy thing", was the work of God.

Without a doubt, the promised seed was a fertilized human egg which came from heaven. It is important to emphasize that the fertilized egg (seed) was not Christ. The fertilized human egg (seed) was a new creation. This seed would develop to become the physical body of the second Adam (Man). Scriptures make it plain that the physical body came first and then the spiritual. See 1 Corinthians 15: 45-46.

The heavenly supplied seed that was to form the body of Jesus, contained identical genetic codes to those of Adam. The seed was of the same biological composition as the seed of man. The number of chromosomes and all chemical elements were the same as in Adam.

Virgin Mary's Pregnancy

Thousands of years passed from the day Adam sinned until the promise of the redeemer was fulfilled. The fullness of time came 2,030 years ago when God chose the woman to bear the seed. God chose the virgin Mary, who was a descendant of King David. She was the espoused wife of Joseph. Joseph of the tribe of Judah was in a direct line to the throne of David.

Mary's pregnancy was a unique gestational event. The way she was conceived was different from that of a normal human conception. Mary's egg was not used in her conception. Neither was a gamete from a man used.

The Redeemer

The Redeemer's physical body was divinely planned before the foundation of the world. God planned His body for a two-fold purpose. Firstly, it was to be the holy tabernacle to house the Spirit of God; and secondly, it was to be sacrificed for the sin of mankind.

The Scriptures declare that it was not possible for the blood of animals to atone for sins. Consequently, when Jesus came into the world He said, "Sacrifice and offering thou wouldest not, but a body hast thou prepared me: Lo I come to do thy will, O God."[20] This statement highlights the reason for Christ's coming in a bodily form. He came to offer Himself as the perfect sacrificial lamb. This was required by God for atonement for the sin of man.

The physical body of Jesus was an entirely new creation. The "holy thing" developed in Mary's womb was the last Adam (man).[21] The first man (Adam) came from earthly materials, but the last man came from heavenly materials. Nonetheless, the second man had identical human genes. But, unlike the first Adam, He was pure, holy and undefiled.

Chapter 4: Angelic Annunciations

The fullness of time came when God would fulfill His promise to send the Prophet/Redeemer into the world. King Herod was ruler of Judea while the Roman Emperor, Caesar Augustus was overlord of the Jews. In about the year 11BCE God sent the angel Gabriel to Nazareth to deliver a message to Mary. Mary was at that time engaged to Joseph.

It was early in the morning. Mary started her day with prayers and supplications to God. She finished praying and looked towards the window in her bedroom. She was startled at the sudden appearance of an angel in the far side of the room. She was petrified. She froze, and was visibly shaking with fear.

The angel Gabriel observed her nervousness, and distress. He smiled reassuringly. He immediately calmed Mary with a warm and friendly greeting. He told her that she was endowed with God's grace and favor. The angel then proposed an offer to Mary. The offer required Mary's full agreement and cooperation. The offer can be described as a gestational contract.

The essence of the contract was that God chose Mary to bear a son. Creator God would provide the seed (fertilized egg). He would then miraculously place the seed into Mary's womb.

The angel told Mary that she would conceive, and become pregnant. The holy thing would then develop in her womb, and she would give birth to a son. Finally, she must name him JESUS, and He shall be called the Son of God.

Observe that Mary was given no biological or physiological part in the contract. Her only role was to be the vessel to contain the seed. Subsequently, Mary asked how she could get pregnant without a man. The angel explained to her that her pregnancy would be a miracle performed by the Holy Spirit. In essence, the Lord would supply a seed (holy thing), and supernaturally place it into Mary's womb to initiate the pregnancy.

Mary was still confused and could not understand the mechanism of that great miracle. The angel then told her the story of her baren aunt Elizabeth, and how she miraculously conceived in her old age, and was now in her sixth month of pregnancy.

After hearing the testimony of the angel Gabriel, Mary was now convinced that miracles do happen. She understood the message of the conception. Subsequently, she voluntarily agreed to the verbal contract as presented by the angel. She submitted her will and her whole being as a vessel to be used by God.

The angel's report that Elizabeth was in her 6th month of pregnancy, indicates that Elizabeth got pregnant in April that year. Therefore, Gabriel's visit with Mary took place in the month of Tishrei/September, and most likely at the time of Yom Kippur ("Day of Atonement") 10th Tishrei, 3751 – Hebrew calendar. This would be September 15th, 11BCE on the Gregorian calendar.

The angel ended his visit and left as suddenly as he came. It is very likely that the Spirit of God went to Mary's home in Nazareth, soon after Gabriel's visit ended. Mary was alone at home. Most likely the Shekinah Glory of the Lord filled the house.

The Scriptures state that the Holy Spirit overpowered the Virgin Mary, and probable caused her to fall into a deep sleep. The Holy Spirit then miraculously placed the Seed (fertilized egg) into Mary's womb. There was no involvement of carnality, and no human element was involved in the process of Mary's conception.

Not long after the angel visited Mary, she discovered that she was pregnant. She got very excited about the prospect of having a baby.

She wanted to share the news with someone. But there was no one in Nazareth that she could trust. She had been a resident in Nazareth for only a short period of time, and had no close friends.

Mary had no one in Nazareth with whom she could trust to share such an intimate story. Moreover, no one would believe her. And since she was espoused to be married, sharing such news would have placed her life in jeopardy. She would be wrongfully accused of adultery and stoned to death. She even refused to share it with Joseph at that time.

Mary probably reasoned that only one person in the world would understand and believe her story, her aunt Elizabeth. She would believe because her conception was also announced by the angel Gabriel.

Moreover, Mary had that burning desire to see her elderly pregnant aunt. She also wanted to tell her own story of Gabriel's visitation. However, there was one problem: Elizabeth was living in the hill country of Hebron, which was a very far distance from Nazareth.

The Bible identifies that hill country as a location in Judah, and the town as Hebron, a city allocated to the priests.[22] Centuries earlier when Joshua divided the conquered lands, he gave the town of Hebron to the descendants of Aaron.

The distance from Nazareth to Elizabeth's home was about 85 miles. However, the desire to see Elizabeth was so strong, that the distance was no obstacle to the young, exuberant, and energetic maiden.

Mary arrived at Elizabeth's home and found her pregnant, just as the angel had told her. Elizabeth believed Mary's story of her miraculous conception. She rejoiced with her for the favor and blessings that God bestowed on her niece. Mary stayed at Hebron for three months.[23] She returned to Nazareth in January, after Elizabeth gave birth.

While Mary was away in Hebron, Joseph was planning for the big wedding festivities. He was unaware that his espoused wife was about three months pregnant.

Mary returned to her residence in Nazareth about the second week in January. She could no longer hide her pregnancy from Joseph and planned to discuss the matter with him. She privately told her husband about the angel's visit with her, and explained the angel's message regarding her miraculous pregnancy. Furthermore, she told Joseph that she willingly agreed to get pregnant.

Joseph was shocked by the news, bewildered by what his fiancée told him and he immediately came to a rash conclusion. He believed that Mary was unfaithful while she was away at Hebron.

Joseph knew that it takes two to make a baby. He reasoned that a man must have been involved. Joseph did not believe a single word of his fiancées' story. He was angry, perplexed, confused, and emotionally hurt. He reasoned that she must have slept with a man because there is no other way a woman can get pregnant except by the carnal method.

That night, Joseph could not fall asleep. He thought long and hard on how to deal with this serious marriage crisis. He desired to find a way to get out of the marriage. He wanted to get out fast but without causing much embarrassment to his family. At the same time, he did not wish to expose Mary to public disgrace. That would expose her to danger. Under Jewish law, she would be accused of adultery and stoned to death.

After long agonizing sleepless hours Joseph finally arrived at amicable solution. It was a resolution that he thought was in Mary's best interest. He concluded that it was best to secretly dissolve the betrothal contract. He would then send her away clandestinely before her pregnancy was visible.

After deciding the matter in his mind, he fell asleep. That night, the angel of the Lord appeared to Joseph in a dream. The angel of the Lord told Joseph that he should not be afraid to take Mary home as his wife, because her conception was the work of the Holy Spirit. The angel of the Lord further told him that Mary would give birth to a son.

The angel of the Lord commanded Joseph not to have any intimate relationship with Mary until after she gave birth to her first-born child. The Lord further commanded Joseph to name the child JESUS because He would save His people from their sins.

That dream confirmed everything that Mary had told Joseph, and he became satisfied that she was not unfaithful. Joseph obeyed the angel of the Lord. He went for Mary and took her in marriage. He then brought her to his house, but he never had any intimate relations with her until after she gave birth to her first son, Jesus.[24]

Chapter 5 In the Fullness of Time

The event of the birth of Jesus is undoubtedly the most researched and discussed event recorded in the Scriptures. There are many skeptics who pour scorn and ridicule on the holy event. Likewise, there are many people who do not believe the Scriptures concerning the nativity narrative.

There are many who are still searching for proof that Jesus was born in Bethlehem 2,000 years ago. The gospel of Matthew says that Jesus was born at the time of a Roman empire-wide census registration, when Herod was king.

The first census that was decreed by Augustus took place in 28BCE. There were two more empire-wide censuses. Two of those censuses took place during the reign of Herod the Great.

Gospel writer Luke wrote that Quirinius was governor when Jesus was born. However, the year of the census when Quirinius was governor of Syria has been the subject of debates for many centuries.

There seem to be no consensus as to the year of the census when Jesus was born. Consequently, dates ranging from 8BCE to CE1 has been suggested. An accurate date for the nativity census is the key to determine the correct year when Jesus was born. Yet, there are undeniable historical accounts and archeological findings that pin-point the exact year of the birth of Jesus. Nonetheless, placing the birth in the correct year has proven very problematic for scholars.

A Divine Mystery

A Wikipedia encyclopedia entry on the accuracy of the dating of the birth of Jesus, quoted Doggart saying that although scholars generally believe that Christ was born sometime before CE1, the historical evidence is too sketchy to allow for a definitive dating of the event.

The gospel writers Matthew and Luke both recorded the time of the birth of Jesus relative to the reign of King Herod of Judea. They also stated that Jesus was born at the time of the Roman empire-wide census.

Matthew wrote that Jesus was born in Bethlehem, Judea, during the reign of King Herod the Great. Matthew's date ranged over a period of thirty-seven years, which was the length of the reign of King Herod. On the other hand, Luke narrowed the time down to weeks during the census registration.

Luke wrote to Theophilus and informed him that the letter was based upon eyewitnesses that were living during that time. Luke wrote with confidence and stated the facts as he received them.

Luke presented the nativity with boldness, writing, "And it came to pass in those days, that there went out a decree from Caesar Augustus, that all the world should be taxed. (And the taxing was first made when Cyrenius was governor of Syria) And all went to be taxed every one into his own city."[25]

Matthew's account of the time of the nativity is more readily accepted by many people. On the other hand, Luke's account generates questions, and is very controversial. This is because there seems to be no historical account of Cyrenius as governor of Syria, during the reign of Herod when Jesus was said to be born.

Skeptics and unbelievers demand historical verification of Luke's nativity narrative. Their demand seems more like a challenge to the authenticity of the word of God rather than a challenge to Luke. The scripture is the word of God. The Bible declares that "All scripture is given by inspiration of God."[26]

God is the author of the Scriptures; He inspired the writers. The writers were merely the men with the pen, who records the things that the Lord impress upon their minds. Luke wrote under the inspiration of the Holy Spirit; therefore, his narrative is true.

God is sovereign. He rules by fiat from His throne in Heaven. The Lord determines all thing, and all times and events, according to His divine plan and purpose. Accordingly, God set a date, time and place for the birth of His Son Jesus. God then revealed that divinely set date to His servants, the prophets, who recorded them in the Bible.

The predetermined time for Christ to come into the world came two thousand years ago. Since then, bible scholars have tried to determine the correct year of Jesus' birth with no success. Nevertheless, the year of the birth of Jesus is not a great mystery.

Both secular history and religious records possess ample evidence which gave a definitive time of the birth of Jesus. There are many undisputable accounts that prove that the gospel writers were correct in their portrayal of the nativity narrative, and that the word of God is true.

Chapter 6
Intervening Politics

The Roman census under Augustus Caesar comes to mind when determining the time of Jesus' birth. The census is the key that will unlock the mystery year of the birth of Jesus. The purpose of the census was to number all the citizens and people, under the authority of the Roman Government. The census covered the provinces in which individuals were assessed and taxed, as well as client states that paid tribute.

Judea was a client state until 6CE, and as such, paid tribute to Rome. Under the tribute system, the Jews were individually assessed but did not pay direct taxation to Rome. However, they were required to take the census so that the Roman government could assess the wealth of their country in order to determine the tribute valuation.

During Augustus' long reign of over forty years, only three empire-wide censuses were attributed to him. Prior to the start of the censuses, the emperor appointed special officers, and sent them into the provinces, and territories to conduct the registration.

The responsibility of the census organizer was sometimes discharged by imperial legati.[27] These census officers were assisted by subordinates called censuales, who actually make out the lists. Staff organization, training, and provincial preparation usually take a few months from the time the census is decreed, until the registration begins.

The census decreed by Augustus when Jesus was born, required that all people be registered in their tribal homeland. This was required so as to get an accurate count of each tribe in the empire.

Archeology Evidence

The empire-wide censuses decreed by Augustus were recorded on the document called "*Res Gestae Augustus*" – the deeds of the divine Augustus. The document was written by Augustus before he died, and read in the Senate along with his will. The original tablets on which the Deeds of Augustus were inscribed were lost or destroyed, after the fall of the Roman Empire.

About 1555CE, a Dutch scholar visiting Ancyra in Asia Minor discovered a copy of the document, on white marble on the walls of a temple. The tablets were severely damaged, and parts were missing. It was therefore difficult to reconstruct the sentences, and replicate the original information accurately.

Several attempts were made to restore the document, and as a result of the work of a German historian named Christian Moomsen, a completed copy was published in 1883. That document was named "*Momumentum Ancyranum*" – the deeds of Augustus.

The document produced by Moomsen was composed from a damaged tablet that had missing fragments; consequently, the missing words of the text were inserted by Moomsen based on prevailing knowledge in 1883.

In chapter eight of the document, Augustus mentioned three general censuses that he decreed. Moomsen's reconstructed document states that in his sixth consulate (28BCE) Augustus made a census of the people with Marcus Agrippa as his colleague. Then again, with consular imperium Augustus conducted a lustrum alone when Gaius Censorinus and Gaius Asinius were consuls (8BCE), Moomsen surmised.

Moomsen's date of 8BCE was most likely an assumed date that he interjected to fill the missing gap in the text due to the damaged fragment of the original document.

Moomsen mentions a third empire-wide census when Augustus with consular imperium, conducted the lustrum with Tiberius as his colleague. This took place when Sextus Pompeius and Sextus Appuleius were consuls (14BCE).

First century Roman historian Gaius Suetonius, who was born in 70CE and lived during the glory days of Rome, described three censuses that were decreed by Augustus. Roman historian Suetonius documented them in his book, *The Lives of 12 Caesars – Life of Augustus*. Suetonius most certainly had seen and read the original bronze tablet called the *"Res Gestae Devi Augusti"* in front of Augustus' Mausoleum.

Suetonius confirmed the decree of the three censuses, but he did not attempt to date them. He wrote that "three times he (Augustus) took the census of the Roman people, the first and third times with a colleague, the second time alone."[28]

Suetonius' historical statement validated Moomsen's entry of the number of times the census was taken without affirming the dates. The three historical dates for Augustus' nation-wide censuses were also documented by 2nd century Roman historian Cassius Dio. He was the son of a Roman senator. Dio spent twenty-two years researching, and compiling a complete history of the Roman Empire in eighty volumes.

Like Suetonius, Dio had seen and read the Res Gestae in Rome. Dio wrote that in his sixth consulate (28BCE) Augustus became censor with Agrippa as his colleague. That entry matches the recording on Moomsen's restored document. Regarding the third census, Dio wrote that "Augustus sent men out everywhere to make a list of the properties both of private individuals, and cities."[29] According to Dio, the time of the third census took place when Lucius Munatius and Gaius Sillius had been installed as consuls in 13CE.[30]

Dio gave the reason why Augustus decreed the census of 13CE. He wrote that a dispute arose in the senate objecting to Augustus' imposition of a 5% tax hike. In an effort to avoid any censure of himself, Caesar deliberated with Tiberius and his counselors.

He then switched from the proposed 5% tax increase, and decreed a general census. Dio wrote in chapter twenty-nine that Augustus died at Nola the following year, 14CE, when Sextus Apuleius and Sextus Pompeius were consuls.[31]

Dio's record of a third Augustus decreed census in 13CE, conflicts with Moomsen's date of 14CE. Moomsen's reconstructed *Momumentum Ancyranum* document dated the second census at 8 BCE, during the consularship of Gaius Censorinus and Gaius Asinius. However, neither Cassius Dio nor another great Roman historian named Titius Livius who was alive at that time (59 BCE-17CE), seem to validate Moomsen's reconstructed documented date for the second census. Neither did Suetonius validate Moomsen's 8BCE census date. Suetonius simply did not include a date.

Moomsen apparently guessed the date of the second census, because portions of the Res Gestae Divi Augusti Monument were missing, due to damages. Dio on the other hand provided historical evidence with verifiable written accounts from which the date of the second census can easily be extracted.

In book 54, Dio wrote that P. Sulpicius Quirinius and C. Valgius Rufus was elected consuls (12BCE), and that year Augustus' son-in-law Agrippa died.

Augustus would not have his daughter become a lonely widow, raising his two grandsons by herself. Therefore, he forced Tiberius to divorce his pregnant wife. She was also raising another small child at that time. Augustus then betrothed his daughter Julia, widow of Agrippa, to Tiberius. He then immediately dispatched him to the war zone in Pannonia in the spring of 11BCE.

Augustus' step-son Drusus, and the brother of Tiberius, was appointed praetor urbanus in the counsellorship of Quintas Aelius and Paulus Fabius 11BCE. At the beginning of spring, that year, Drusus on orders from Caesar left Rome, and travelled to Germany to conduct war against the tribes east of the river Rhine. As the year came to a close and winter began to set in, Drusus withdrew his army and returned to Rome.

Drusus was supposed to conduct the fall festivals that year, but did not return to Rome on time. The historian Dio wrote that the festivals belonging to Drusus' praetorship was managed by someone else.

A Divine Mystery

The festivals pertained to Augustus' birthday, which was celebrated throughout the empire every year during the month of September. The festival was named the Augustalia in honor of Augustus whose birthday was on September 23. He was celebrating his 52nd birthday that year, 11BCE.

While the birthday festivities were taking place, Tiberius was fighting a war against the Pannonians and the Dalmatians. At the same time, an uprising broke out in Thrace. This prompted Augustus to immediately order Lucius Piso, the governor of Pamphylia, to proceed to Thrace to quell the rebellion.[32]

Augustus then dispatched Quirinus to Asia to succeed Piso as governor of Pamphylia and Galactica. And problems keep popping up everywhere. Meanwhile, on the home front Augustus' sister Octavia died. Historian Cassius Dio wrote that all the aforementioned events occurred during the consulship of Quintas Aelius Tuberto and Paulus Fabius Maximus in 11BCE.

Augustus seemed overwhelmed with the avalanche of events. While all these events were occurring (in 11BCE), Augustus decreed a census.[33] This was the census that Augustus decreed by himself because Agrippa, his top adviser, had died months earlier, and Tiberius, his new top adviser, and adopted son and heir apparent, was at war in Pannonia. The historian Dio indicated that Augustus decreed the census after his birthday celebrations ended in September, 11BCE.

What prompted Augustus to make such an irrational, and consequential political decision without an advisor at his side at that time remains a mystery. It hardly makes sense why Augustus made such a decree at a time like that. Surely, it was not a good time to take a census in the waring provinces.

There was rebellion everywhere in the empire. All his top generals were at war fighting to suppress the rebellious provinces. To decree a census and tax hike on all citizens in an empire in turmoil is like adding insult to injury. Moreover, the census was decreed to take place within a twelve-month time frame.

Soon after Augustus made the decree, one of his generals, Drusus returned from war. This was after the festivals were over. Augustus immediately appointed him as Censor, and chief administrator of the census.[34] Drusus planned and organized the empire-wide census over the next few months.

Census officers were placed throughout the empire, and registration began in the spring of the following year - 10BCE. The registration began in March and continued until the end of spring sometime in June.

Cassius Dio confirms that the census took place in 10BCE, the year before Drusus died. Drusus died 9BCE from injuries he received when he accidently fell from his horse.[35] These recorded historical facts are indisputable. Again, this date of the 10BCE census differs from Moomsen's 8BCE, arrived at from the reconstructed, and damaged document of the deeds of Augustus.

Nonetheless, the majority of documented historical records by first and second century historians, strongly suggest that the dates for the Augustus decreed censuses were 28 BCE, 10BCE and 13CE.

Chapter 7
Quirinius

Luke, the gospel writer, introduced the nativity of our Lord Jesus Christ by stating unequivocally that Jesus was born during the time of the Roman empire-wide census, when Quirinius was governor of Syria. Matthew simply recorded that Jesus was born in Bethlehem, in Judea, during the reign of Herod.

Matthew's account is universally accepted, but Luke's account generates some questions of authenticity. Needless to say, Luke's writing of the nativity is proven to be among the most controversial Scriptures in the Christian Bible.

Many people are offended by it because they find no independent verification of the Augustus tax event at the time of Jesus' birth. Neither were any found that indicate that Quirinius was governor of Syria at the time when Jesus was born.

Both the Scriptures and recorded secular history mentioned a census in Judea in 6CE. However, that was not an empire-wide census at the time of the nativity. The 6CE census was called after Augustus banished King Archelaus, and decreed Judea a province of Rome. The census was specifically for Judea, after it became an imperial province. As a consequence, the tax system for Judea immediately changed. This change necessitated an immediate tax assessment. Consequently, the national tribute system, was replaced by an individual direct taxation system.

Quirinius

Jesus was born before Herod's death. History records that Herod died in 4BCE. Quirinius was governor of Syria in 6CE. Since Jesus was born before Herod died, then Quirinius must have been Governor of Syria before 4BCE. However, there were no records of Quirinius as governor of Syria prior to 6CE. This leads many scholars, and skeptics to conclude that Luke made an error in dating the birth of Jesus.

In his narrative, Luke wrote that his source of information was from direct testimonies of eyewitnesses, who were living at the time when Jesus was born in Bethlehem.

Moreover, he accompanied Paul on his mission to Jerusalem in 52-53CE. While there he interviewed many people, who recalled the event of the nativity. They remembered hearing the shepherds as they proclaimed that the Savior, Christ the Lord was born in Bethlehem. Those people also remembered the census at the time, as well as the name of the governor who was in charge of the registration. In his narrative, Luke wrote that he carefully investigated all the testimonies of the nativity.

At this time, it is worthwhile to observe Quirinius' connection to Caesar Augustus, as well as the census that is the source of the controversy. We also researched historical evidence to corroborate Luke's story so as to vindicate the gospel writer. We will also follow Quirinius' path to his position as Governor of Syria.

In 15BCE, Caesar Augustus appointed Quirinius as governor of the province of Crete and Cyrene. In 12BCE, he was elected Consul, the highest elected office in the Roman Government. The Roman historian Livius wrote that Augustus appointed Quirinius as governor of Galatia and Pamphylia in Asia, in 11BCE to succeed Governor Piso.

While in Asia, Quirinius fought against the Homonadensians. The historian Tactus, did not ignore Quirinius' victory over the Homonadenses at that time, so he gave him credit for it. The historian thereby proves that Quirinius was governor of the region at that time.[36]

The historian Strabo also wrote about the Homnadensesian war and recorded that Quirinius was the commanding General. Strabo recorded that he overthrew the inhabitants by starving them, and capturing four thousand men alive, settling them in neighboring cities.

Quirinius returned to Rome, and was given another victory parade called 'Triumph'.

Strabo's book, *Geographia,* was completed, and the first edition was published in 7 BCE. The Homonadensen war took place in 11 BCE, and proves that Quirinius was in close proximity to Judea during the war.

In his later years, Quirinius fell out of favor with the powerful Roman elite, who suppressed most of his achievements. The Roman historians left only a sparse record of him. However, funerary (memorial) stones tracked his pathway in the eastern provinces of the Roman Empire, and marked his stops, and recorded his achievements.

The Antioch Stones

In 1912 and 1913 CE, two memorial stones that provided concrete evidence of Quirinius' service in Asia Minor were found. They were discovered in two Muslim villages in the vicinity of Pisidian Antioch. The first stone mentioned Gaius Caristanius Fronto as Prefect, serving under Publius Sulpicius Quirinius the Duumvir (Chief Magistrate).

The stone was not dated, which makes it difficult to tell the exact date of Quirinius' service as Duumvir. Nevertheless, the events that led to the making of the monument can be easily traced. We know from the records that Lucius Piso was Governor of Pamphylia until 11 BCE, and was ordered by Augustus to quell a rebellion in Thrace.[37] At that time, 11 BCE, Piso was planning the war strategy against the Homonadensians in the Pisidian Mountains.

Quirinius was elected Consul in 12 BCE. The deployment of Piso created an opening for a high-level military commander in the Galatia Province. The sudden departure of Piso in 11 BCE allowed Caristanius Fronto, who was appointed Prefect, to manage the affairs of the province temporarily.

However, a more powerful military leader was required. Consequently, Augustus appointed Quirinius with full Imperium Legati (governor), and dispatched him to Galatia to execute the war against the

Homonadensians. The Antioch memorial stone confirms Livius' statement that Quirinius was appointed governor of Galatia/Pamphylia.

The second Pisidian stone came from the base of a statue, and it revealed some very important information. The statue was erected by the family of Fronto by the authority of Marcus Servilius. The stone was in honor of Gaius Caristanius Fronto. The writing on the stone revealed that Fronto was Prefect under the command of Publicius Sulpicius Quirinius the Duumvir.

At the time of the nation-wide census in 10BCE, Augustus appointed Quirinius as Duumvir, and dispatched him to Syria. Duumvir is defined as one of two Roman officers or magistrates united in the same public function – in this instance, as governor with equal authority.

Observe that Marcus Titius was governor of Syria at that time. However, Augustus appointed Quirinius as Imperial Legate (Duumvir), and as a commanding officer over one legion, dispatched him to Syria. Quirinius orders were temporary, and was limited to the census operations in the region.

His orders were specifically to suppress any rebellion, and to keep the peace during the time of the 10BCE census registration. Because Quirinius was stationed in Syria, and dealt directly with Judea, the people regarded him as the governor of Syria.

Though not recorded by the Roman historians, Quirinius' service in Syria was clearly written on memorial (tomb) stones. One such stone is the Lapis Venetus Aemilius Secundus memorial stone. This stone was found in Venice in 1674. The stone is said to have been acquired in Beirut, Lebanon, by a merchant of Venice, and it was later taken to Venice.

The inscription on the stone states that Quirinius was legate of the imperial province of Syria, and was the military officer in command during the empire-wide census. A legate was a deputy governor of an imperial province, who is appointed by Caesar as a legionary commander for a specific duty.

The Venice stone is not dated, but it lends credibility to the idea that there were two censuses in the Syrian province while Quirinius was in that region. First was the empire-wide census when Jesus was born, and the 6CE census when Judea became an imperial province of Rome.

The inscription on the stone reads: Quintus Aemilius Secundus, son of Quintus, of the Palatine Tribe (which served) in the army of the divine Augustus, under P. Sulpicius Quirinius, Caesar's legate in Syria, decorated with honors, prefect of the 1st Augusta cohort and prefect of the 2nd Classica cohort. Moreover, by order of Quirinius, I carried out a census of one hundred and seventeen thousand citizens from the city of Apamea.

Moreover, dispatched on a mission by Quirinius against the Ituraeans of Mount Liban, I took their citadel. And before military service, (I was) prefect of the labourers and seconded by two consuls to the "aerarium." And in the colony, questor, aedile on two occasions, duumvir on two occasions and pontiff. Here is buried Q. Aemilius Secundus son of Quintus, of the Palatine tribe (my) son and Chia (my) emancipated slave. This monument is excluded from the inheritance.

This Secundus monument attests to the fact that Quirinius was indeed a military commander in Syria for the purpose of keeping the peace in the province, and adjoining territories during the census of 10BCE.

However, Quirinius was not the administrative governor. The governor of Syria at that time was Marcus Titius who served from 12BCE to 9BCE. Titius was succeeded by Gaius Sentius Saturninus, who was recalled in 6CE, and Augustus appointed Quirinius as his successor.[38]

This 10BCE empire-wide census must not be confused with the 6CE census. The 6CE census was decreed for Judea only, after the banishment of Herod Archelaus. Prior to 6CE, Judea was a client state of Rome, and as such paid tribute to Rome. However, Judea became a province in 6CE, and the taxing system changed from a national tribute system to an individual taxation system. As a result, Augustus ordered a tax assessment for the new province.

Note that Quirinius was featured in both censuses. Firstly, as a legate (assisting governor) of Syria and commanding general with orders to keep the peace during the empire-wide census registration in

10BCE. Secondly, Quirinius was the administrative governor of Syria in 6CE. when Judea became a province, and was annexed to Syria.

These historical and archaeological records prove beyond the shadow of a doubt that Cyrenius (Quirinius) was in Syria at the time of the Augustus-decreed empire-wide census registration of 10BCE. Surely, these records should vindicate the gospel writer Luke. The historical facts should put to rest the dispute regarding Quirinius as governor of Syria, and the time of the empire-wide census when Jesus was born.

Chapter 8 — More Evidences

Another extra-Biblical source that dates the Augustus tax decree at 11BCE is the Arabic Infancy Gospel-Apocrypha (New Testament) – Christianity. Chapter two of The Arabic Infancy Gospel records the following: "In the three hundred and ninth (309th) year of the era of Alexander, Augustus put forth an edict that every man should be enrolled in his native place.

Joseph therefore arose, taking Mary his spouse, they went away to Jerusalem and came to Bethlehem, to be enrolled along with his family in his native city." (Source: *'The Arabic Gospel of the Infancy of the Savior' as translated by Alexander Roberts and James Donaldson*.)

Jerusalem was captured by Ptolemy Soter, a general of Alexander the Great, in 320BCE. Subsequently, the census was decreed in the 309 years after Alexandrian (Greek) rule began in Jerusalem; and not from the time when Alexander the Great began his reign. With reference to the Gregorian calendar, the 309th year of Alexander is dated at 11BCE. (320-309)

Birth-year revealed by the prophet

There are two passages of Scriptures from which the correct date can be extracted. The first passage in the book of Daniel. The angel Gabriel appeared to the prophet in Babylon during the time when Judah was in Babylonian captivity. During that appearance, Gabriel gave Daniel a prophetic message concerning the time of the birth of Jesus.

The angel said: "Know therefore and understand, that from the going forth of the commandment to restore and build Jerusalem until the Messiah the prince shall be seven weeks, and three scores and two weeks: the street shall be built again, and the wall, even in troublous times. And after three scores and two weeks shall Messiah be cut off, but not for himself."[39] 'Weeks' in this prophecy literally means weeks of years, or one week equals seven years.

The prophecy was fulfilled by Persian kings. The time to restore and build Jerusalem was given by two Persian kings in two segments of time. The first order to restore Jerusalem was given by King Cyrus in 538BCE. At that time, King Cyrus emancipated the Jews, and decreed that that they return to Jerusalem, and build the Temple. That first block of time was seven weeks (49 years). Thousands of Jews accepted the king's clemency and returned to Judah under the leadership of Zerubbabel, and they built the Temple.[40]

A second Persian king issued a decree to rebuild the walls of Jerusalem. The order was given by King Artaxerxes in the twentieth year of his reign in 444BCE.[41] Artaxerxes ascended to the throne in 464BCE.[42]

The king appointed Nehemiah to be governor of Judea in 434 BCE. He then dispatched him with full authority to rebuild the city of Jerusalem. This decree was issued ninety-four years after that of King Cyrus.

Observe that the date of the decree 434BCE marked the starting point of Daniel's sixty-two-week prophecy concerning Messiah. That segment of the prophecy was predicted to end in the year of the coming of the Messiah.[43] Daniel's predicted time of four hundred and thirty-four years for the coming of Messiah ended at 10BCE, (444BCE, time of decree less 434 years). Note that 10BCE was the year of the Roman empire-wide tax registration when Quirinius was governor of Syria.

Chapter 9
Preview of the Nativity

The Lord ordered the birth of Jesus for a specific date, time and place. God revealed the year to his prophet Daniel more than four hundred and thirty years prior to the holy event. God not only revealed the year of the nativity, but He also made known the place where Jesus would be born. The Jewish prophet Micah predicted that the place of birth would be Bethlehem, in Judea.[44]

As the appointed time approached, the Lord prepared the way for the birth of Jesus. God sent the angel Gabriel to Jerusalem during the week of Passover, Nisan 14th. Gabriel had a message from God for priest Zacharias. Zacharias ministered at the Temple sanctuary during that Passover week.

Zacharias was pouring oil in the lamps when the angel Gabriel suddenly appeared. Zacharias saw the angel, and was scared. The angel spoke and told Zacharias that his wife Elizabeth will conceive and have a male child. Zacharias did not believe because his wife was old.

Gabriel struck him with dumbness because he refused to accept the message from God, and he instantly lost his voice because of his unbelief. Although he could not speak, Zacharias continued with his assignment. His service in the Temple was for the month of Nissan. As soon as the month ended, he returned to his home in Hebron.

Soon after he went home, slept with his wife Elizabeth and she conceived. The angel's word was quickly fulfilled. Elizabeth got pregnant in the month of Iyar/April.

A Confused Emperor

Meanwhile, at the power base in Rome, Emperor Augustus was overwhelmed with a host of problems. No news was good news for him. There were uprisings on several fronts of the empire. The Roman armies were everywhere, fighting to suppress the rebellions. In the midst of the chaos, his son-in-law and chief adviser died suddenly. His daughter was left a widow with two young children. Soon after, his sister passed away. All those tragedies occurred in 11BCE, the year of his 52nd birthday.

Alone and confused, Augustus on the spur of the moment decreed a census. He commanded that everyone in his empire must register for the census in his tribal city.

There was no apparent reason for thousands of people living far from their tribal cities to return home only to be registered for a census. The decree given in that manner guaranteed the birth of Jesus in the city of David.

Undoubtedly, Augustus decree was divinely inspired, and timed to fulfill God's purpose and plan. All people are servants of the Lord, and he uses anyone whether they are bad or good to accomplish his plans. The Scriptures rightly says that the king's heart is in the hand of the Lord, and he can cause the king to do whatever He wills.[45]

Augustus decreed the census sometime in September 11BCE, during the time of his month-long 52nd birthday celebrations. In that same month, the Lord sent the angel Gabriel to Nazareth, Israel. The angel announced to Mary that God chose her to bear the holy seed. The angel also told Mary that her aunt Elizabeth was in her sixth month of pregnancy.

Observe that Gabriel did not say that Elizabeth was in the 6th (Hebrew) month, but rather in her 6th month. Therefore, the counting of her pregnancy month did not begin the first month - Nisan/March. The reason is that Zacharias was serving in the Temple in Jerusalem that month, while Elizabeth was at home in Hebron, and the couple did not sleep together for the month of Nissan.

Elizabeth's first month of pregnancy was Alyar/April, 11BCE. Therefore, Gabriel's appearance to Mary was in Tishrei/September. The visitation may have been on the Day of Atonement, which is the most sacred day in the life of Israel. It is a day that is devoted to repentance and making supplications to God. Very likely, Mary was praying and making supplications to God when Gabriel suddenly appeared.

It is very likely that on that same day after the angel departed from Mary, the Holy Spirit came and overshadowed Mary. The reason for the invisible God coming into the world was to atone for the sins of man. Therefore, it seems fitting that the holy seed, would be divinely placed in Mary on the Day of Atonement. That holy seed would develop to become the material, undefiled and sinless body of Christ, which was destined to be sacrificed.[46] It is then reasonable to believe that Mary conceived on that sacred Day of Atonement, on the 10th Tishrei 3751 (15th September 11BCE).[47]

Chapter 10 The Night When Jesus Was Born

The time when Jesus was born has been debated for centuries. Yet, there seems to be no consensus as to the time of the blessed world-changing event. Consequently, many different dates have been proposed, ranging from 8 BCE to 1BCE. Notwithstanding, the coming of Christ into the world is the greatest divine event of all times.

The coming of the Lord was predicted by the prophets; and the birth of Jesus was the most anticipated event in the history of Israel. The main reason is because the idea of a Messiah was encoded in the Davidic Covenant. And the Davidic Covenant was established more than a thousand years before Jesus was born.[48] Moreover, the prophet Isaiah predicted the birth of the Christ-child seven hundred and fifty years before His birth.[49]

However, the year of Jesus' birth eluded the great minds for centuries. But the Lord will not have His people ignorant as to that sacred date of the birth of his Son. It is said that what is hidden from the wise and the prudent will be revealed to the babes and suckling.

The Augustus decreed census registration was due to begin in the Spring of 10BCE. Likewise, the Passover was in the Spring. The decreed census registration of the Davidic clan was to take place in their tribal homeland of Bethlehem. Joseph was therefore forced by the law of man to go to Bethlehem with his wife Mary, to register for the census.

The census registration always take place over the entire Spring months. On the other hand, the feast of the Passover was for a specific date. The Passover was on Nisan 14, 3751 (April 15th 10BCE). Joseph decided to attend the Passover that year, and then proceed to Bethlehem to register for the census.

Mary was in her seventh month of pregnancy, when she and Joseph left Nazareth to journey to Bethlehem. They travelled by way of the Jordan valley towards Jericho. The journey was about seventy-two miles. The road was winding with steep hills and rough dusty stone surfaces. They travelled on foot for about 10 days. The journey was very exhaustive, and it took a toll on the advanced pregnant Mary.

The couple along with other family members arrived at Jerusalem about the second week of April. They stayed over in Jerusalem for the Passover and then continued to Bethlehem. Joseph searched for a place to stay, but could not find any apartment in Bethlehem. All guest rooms were occupied by the pilgrims who had come to the Passover.

The only available vacancy in Bethlehem was a cave on the outskirts of the town. Without any hesitation, Joseph took possession of the cave. He then got to work and used his carpenter skills to make it habitable.

Mary and Joseph moved into the cave-home as soon as it was ready. They reckoned that it would be unwise for Mary to travel back to Nazareth in her advanced state of pregnancy. He then decided to stay in Bethlehem until Mary gave birth. This fact was affirmed by the Scriptures. The Bible records that while they were living in Bethlehem the time came for Mary to deliver her baby. See Luke 2:6.[50] This strongly suggest that pregnant Mary was living in Bethlehem, for a period of time before she gave birth.

Apparently, Joseph wanted Mary to have her baby in the inn, but all the rooms were occupied. They were very disappointed. The baby was on his way, and they quickly returned to their cave-home. Soon thereafter, Mary gave birth to her first son. The mid-wife wrapped the baby in pieces of cloth. She then placed Him on a bed of straws, in a new feeding-trough (manger), which Joseph made.

Decoding Jesus' Birthday

After exhausting biblical and historical research, and examining verifiable historical records and the Scriptures, it is now possible to identify with confidence the year of the empire-wide census, and also the time when Jesus was born in Bethlehem.

The birth year of Jesus as encoded in Daniel's 'Seventy Week' prophecy is 10BCE. Given the historic fact that the nativity census was decreed in September, 11BCE, and that Elizabeth got pregnant in April that year, and Gabriel appeared to Mary in September that same year.

Considering that Gabriel visited Mary on the Day of Atonement, Tishri 10, 3751/September 15, 11BCE, and that she conceived soon thereafter. If this hypothesis is correct, then it is now possible to correctly determine the month and the year when Jesus was born. Given a full gestational term of nine months, the projected month when Jesus was born is Sivan/June 10BCE. All things constant, there is a high degree of probability that Jesus was born between 9th-21st Sivan, 3751 (9th-20th June, 10BCE).[51]

Chapter 11 Bethlehem Shepherds

At the time of Jesus' birth, shepherds were camping out in the late Spring night on the hillside of Bethlehem, watching their flocks. The night-time temperature in Bethlehem in the late spring is usually mild and averages about 72 degrees Fahrenheit. That temperature was comfortable for shepherds to be in an open field, whereas the December temperature averages about 30 degrees at night, which is too cold for shepherds to be out in the open fields all night.

In that calm late Spring night, the shepherds were terrified at the sudden appearance of the angel of the Lord. They sat on the grass, transfixed as the Shekinah glory of the Lord shone around them. They were frightened, and trembled with fear.

The angel of the Lord calmed their fears and told them that he brought good news to the world. He said to them, "Fear not: for, behold, I bring you good tidings of great joy, which shall be to all people. For unto you is born this day in the city of David a Savior, which is Christ the Lord."[52]

The Lord came to Bethlehem on the night when Jesus was born, as a dispenser of grace. This was unlike the divine visit by the Lord on Mount Horeb, when He came as a lawgiver. Instead of speaking to the nation as a whole, he spoke to the shepherds as a representative of the nation. By this act, God signaled a break from the formal religious system established under the Law and established a new order under the direction of Jesus Christ – the Prophet who would speak God's word.[53]

God's message to the shepherds that night, as well as to the Jews, was that the prophet that God promised to them while they were in the wilderness of wanderings many centuries earlier was born in the city of David. The Prophet's name was Jesus Christ (Messiah), the Lord and Savior of the world.

The angel of the Lord implied that Mary's boy child was not an ordinary human being. Divine work was assigned to Him. He was to be Savior, Redeemer, Messiah, the anointed One, and possessor of divine authority and power as Lord.

The angel of the Lord simply announced to the shepherds that Jesus was the Lord from heaven. Suddenly after the angel's announcement, a multitude of angels appeared in the sky. They sung melodious songs of praise to God and announced, "Glory to God in the highest, and on Earth peace, good will towards men."[54]

That night, as soon as the angels departed, the shepherds hurried off to see the baby that the angel spoke of. They came to Bethlehem and saw Mary and Joseph and the baby wrapped in swaddling clothes, and lying on a bed of straw in a feeding trough.

The shepherds were the first people to visit the new-born Son of God - Jesus. They were filled with joy to look at the Savior. It was night, and they left the holy family and went to their homes.

The next day, the shepherds began to proclaim the birth of the Savior in Bethlehem. They went to Jerusalem, which was crowded with people from all over the world. Thousands flocked to the city for the dedication of the rebuilt Temple. The shepherds walked the crowded streets of Jerusalem, and they also went in the Temple. There they proclaimed God's message of the good news of the birth of the Savior of Israel, the Redeemer who is Jesus Christ (Messiah) the Lord.[55] Those lowly shepherds were the first, and earliest recorded evangelists to preach about the Savior Jesus Christ.

Consequently, the news of the birth of Jesus was received by numerous people from different countries who were visiting Jerusalem at that time. On their return home, those visitors spread the news about the birth in Bethlehem of a Savior of Israel who is Christ the Lord.

The shepherds who heard the message from the Lord delivered it to the Jews just as Moses did in the wilderness. Some of those who heard the shepherds preaching were still alive when Luke was writing his gospel, and they were the eyewitnesses that Luke spoke of in the opening remarks of his gospel.

Chapter 12 The Wise Men

Joseph eventually found proper housing for the family. He rented a house in Bethlehem and the family moved into it. Many months passed, and some visitors from a far country came to visit Jesus. Gospel writer Matthew called those visitors "wise men". They were from an eastern nation beyond the Euphrates River. In that time in history there were two great competing empires. There was the Roman Empire which extended from the North Atlantic to the Euphrates River. The next great empire was Parthia. Their land mass extended from the Euphrates River to the Indus River in India. One of their royal cities was Susa, the original capital city of Persia (Iran).

The wise men were most likely astrologers by profession. Undoubtedly, they were residents of Susa, and were astrologers in the king's court. The king of Parthia at that time was Phraates IV. He ruled Parthia from 38BCE until 2BCE. At the same time Augustus Caesar was Emperor of the Roman Empire, and ruled from 31BCE until 14CE.

The people of Judah were familiar with the Parthians. In 40BCE they chased Herod from Judea, and installed Antigonus as king in Jerusalem. However, in 37BCE Herod returned to Jerusalem, and with the help of the Roman army, he deposed King Antigonus. Herod then declared himself king in Jerusalem.

Jesus' Birthday Star

Herod ruled over Judah until his death in 4BCE. Meanwhile in Parthia some astrologers in Susa, Parthia, saw a star of great luminosity in the east. As was customary, they associated the star with a great event taking place on earth. Such stars are usually associated with the birth of great men.

The star was also observed by Chinese astrologers at the same time as the Parthian astrologers. The Chinese recorded the observation in Ho Peng-Yoke 20, catalogue, at number # 62. They called the astrological event a comet, and dated it for June 10BCE. Of interest, the astrologer and mathematician named Ho Peng-Yoke also recorded catalogue # 61, as Halley's Comet in August,12BCE and #63 as a comet in March-April 5BCE and #64 as a comet in April, 4BCE.

Modern scholars accept the Chinese record of catalogues 61, 63, and 64 but rejected catalogue #62 (10BCE) as a ghost event, and a false record. Their reason is that the 10BCE star was not recorded in the Babylonian astronomical catalogue. (*Sources: Collin Humphreys Book - The Star of Bethlehem*)

However, there is no doubt that the star 10BCE was real. The Chinese astrologers saw it and recorded it, same as the astrologers in the Parthian city of Susa. It seems the scholars of today were too hasty in rejecting the documented observation of the comet of 10BCE. The Chinese astrologer should be given the benefit of the doubt, because they were correct in all other observations. It was quite reasonable to believe that the Babylonian astrologers missed the cosmic event of 10BCE.

According to astronomers, the cosmic event in question was most likely a type-1 supernova. It probably exploded at night and observed in China while it was still daylight in Babylon. Type-1 supernovas are very luminous with very high intensity of light, but are transient, and lasts only for a very short time. Scientists say that they may last anywhere from one hour to a few hours' observation. The Babylonians could have missed the event for many reasons. Reasons range from bad

The Wise Men

weather conditions that adversely affected observation of the heavens to the occurrences of the event while it was daylight in Babylon.

Nonetheless, the vigilant Susa astrologers who were hundreds of miles from Babylon observed the event at the same time as the Chinese astrologers. The 10BCE event is therefore credible. It was based on the testimony of two out of three witnesses, namely, the Chinese and the Parthian astrologers in Susa.

The Parthian astrologers were undoubtedly the descendants of Jews who were taken captive to Babylon and Persia centuries earlier. They kept their religion, and knew of the messianic prophecies. They searched the Scriptures and saw the predicted time when Messiah would come to Judea.

Daniel prophesied that from the time of the decree to restore and build Jerusalem unto the Messiah the Prince shall be seven weeks, and then a pause in time, next will be three score and two weeks. Daniel 9: 25. In this prophecy a week is meant to be seven years. The seven weeks (49 years) segment was for the restoring and building of Jerusalem. This was accomplished by Nehemiah.

The three score and two weeks (434 years) was dated from the time of the king's decree. The scripture records that King Artaxerxes of Persia made the decree for the restoration and building of Jerusalem in the twentieth year of his reign. See Nehemiah 2:1. His twentieth regnal year was 444BCE.

The time when the astrologers (wisemen) saw the cosmic event was 10BCE. The prophecy got the astrologers excited. They made a simple calculation (444-434) and discovered that the prophecy of the birth of Messiah the Prince would be in 10BCE.

This seemed to be no coincidence. They reasoned with confidence that the star was the sign of the birth of Messiah, King of the Jews. The three astrologers were ecstatic, and overwhelmed to see how prophecy connects with astrology. They immediately thought of going to Jerusalem to pay homage to the new-born King.

However, they worked in the court of the king, and needed his blessing and permission. The astrologers sought an audience with King

Phraates to inform him of the unusually bright star that they saw in the east.

They told the king about the Messianic prophecies. They then associated the star to the birth of Messiah, the King of the Jews. They impressed upon the king that the birth of the Messiah, King of the Jews was foretold by the Jewish prophets hundreds of years earlier. This was a great moment for the people of Judah, they told the king. They would like to show goodwill to the Jews by visiting Jerusalem. Thereby, the astrologers requested leave to visit the new King in Jerusalem, and to pay homage to the new-born king.

The king showed much interest, and thought it was a worthy mission. King Phraates knew much about Judea. He remembered that his predecessor defeated Herod and installed Antigonus as king in Jerusalem in 40BCE. Three years later, Herod with the help of the Roman army deposed King Antigonus and took the throne.

Phraates regarded the birth of a new king as a good thing for Jerusalem. He approved their request to travel as pilgrims to Jerusalem, and offered to provide all the necessary needs for the journey. The king even offered to provide a cavalry for their protection. King Phraates also pledged to send goodwill gifts to the new-born King. The astrologers were anxious to start their journey.

Unfortunately, they had to delay their travel plans because of diplomatic protocols. At that time Parthia and Rome were sworn enemies. And the road to Jerusalem passes through the Roman province of Syria. Moreover, Judah was a vassal of Rome. The journey to Jerusalem was long and dangerous. The wise-men needed permission from Rome to pass safely through their territories. Phraates, king of Parthia therefore sent a letter to the governor of Syria requesting letters of permission to pass through Syria, and to enter Judea unimpeded.

Augustus eventually granted permission, but it took more than a year before the letters reached the astrologers in Susa. With permission granted, and the blessing of the king, they decided to start their journey in the first week of Spring, 8BCE. King Phraates provided gifts for the new-born king. He gave them a sack of gold, a sack of frankincense, and a sack of myrrh as goodwill gifts to present to the

The Wise Men

King. He provided camels for the astrologists to ride on, and camels to carry their supplies. He also provided a cavalry to escort them safely, along the approximately nine-hundred-mile journey, from Susa to Jerusalem.

The convoy left Susa with the blessings of King Phraates. They departed Susa in March, 8BCE. The astrologists left Susa knowing exactly where they were going, and the purpose of their mission. They absolutely believed that the star of 10BCE indicated that Messiah was born on that June day, according to the timeline of Daniel's prophecy concerning the Messiah. The convoy travelled at the rate of about ten miles each day with rest days for the Sabbath. The journey took about three months. Accordingly, they reached Jerusalem in June.

Upon their entry into the city, the wise men booked into an inn. The next day they went about walking in the city. They visited the newly built Temple, and as they walked about in the city, they asked for the one who was born King of the Jews. They knew very well that Herod was the current reigning king. Yet they confidently asked saying "Where is he that is born King of the Jews? For we have seen his star in the east, and are come to worship him". Matthew 2:2.

The people knew only of Herod as their king, and knew that there was no new-born child in Herod' household. The wise-men no doubt indicated to the people that the new king was Messiah, the Christ, according to the messianic prophecies. The words of the wise-men implied that Messiah was born, and would reign over the Jews.

The words of the wise men certainly caused a stir in the city of Jerusalem. The breaking news of the birth of Messiah spread quickly. The paranoid king Herod was deeply distressed and troubled. He knew that he was an imposter, and he had already purged Judah of all rival aspirants to the throne. Herod had eliminated all the known members of the Hasmonean family who ruled before him. He then turned his attention to the descendants of King David who were the rightful heirs to the throne. He systematically killed all the perceived male Davidic aspirants to the throne. He was shocked to hear that one survived, and was now a threat to his throne. Herod was astounded to hear that such a person was in his midst, even in Jerusalem.

After hearing the news about the child King, Herod consulted with his advisors on the matter. They acknowledged the messianic message of the wise-men. The advisers then informed the king that the Jewish Scriptures foretold of the birth of Christ, the Messiah. Herod was disturbed in his mind. He would have no one challenge him for the throne. With the intention of eliminating all opposition, he forthwith called all the chief priests and scribes, and demanded to know where Christ was to be born. The priests told the king that according to the prophets, the Messiah would be born in Bethlehem, in Judea. Malachi 5:2.

Herod excused the priests and privately called the astrologers. He asked them when did the star first appeared. They told the king that they observed the star in the east at its first appearing in June, two years passed. Herod was satisfied with their candid answer and told them that the child that they sought is in Bethlehem. He further instructed them to return to him, and give him the address so that he, too, could go and worship him.

The Bethlehem Star

The star of Bethlehem has intrigued countless bible scholars over the centuries. Some common explanations for the astronomical event that occurred at the time of Jesus' birth include observation of unusual luminosity events in the heavens. These include the following objects. There was Halley's Comet in 12BCE, a comet observed by the Chinese in 10BCE, a rare triple conjunction of Jupiter and Saturn in 7BCE, a conjunction of Jupiter, Saturn, and Mars in 6BCE, a comet in 5BCE, a comet in 4BCE, and a conjunction of the two brightest stars of Jupiter and Venus 3/2 BCE. Those prominent celestial events took place over a period of 10 years.

There is a degree of difficulty in matching the birth of Jesus with a particular celestial event occurring at the time of a Roman empire-wide census. There were two unknowns in the equation. One relates to the time of the census, and the other to the celestial event.

Halley's Comet of 12BCE was too early because it occurred before the Augustus tax decree. Also, the Jupiter-Venus conjunction of 3/2 BC was too late, given the fact that Herod died in 4BCE, and Jesus was born while Herod was alive.

Since Jesus was born at the time of the census registration of 10BCE, the key is to match the time of Jesus' birth with a documented star observed at the time of the census registration.

The Scriptures affirm that Jesus was born in the year of Augustus' census registration. That was the year the Chinese astrologers observed and documented a very luminous comet. The Chinese comet is the only documented astronomical event that occurred during the Augustus census registration of 10BCE. Therefore, that cosmic event was the star that identified the birth date of Jesus.

There seem to be much misunderstandings and confusion about the Bethlehem star. It is important to know that the star that the astrologers saw in the east was not the Bethlehem star. Firstly, that star was detected when Jesus was born. Observe that two years transpired from the wisemen first saw the star until they arrived in Bethlehem. This fact is recorded in the Scriptures. See Matthew 2:16. Jesus was at that time a toddler, two- years-old.

The star at the time of Jesus' birth only appeared for a brief moment. The time was so short-lived that the Babylonian astrologers missed it. Secondly, that star in the east did not guide the wise-men to Jerusalem. The Scriptures indicated that they knew the messianic prophesies. Accordingly, the astrologers harmonized the year of the star, with the time of the fulfillment of the prophecy of the coming of Messiah the Prince. They knew that Messiah would be born in Judea. They knew where they were going, therefore, there was no need for a star to guide them.

Thirdly, the wisemen did not say that the star guided them to Jerusalem, but only that they observed the star at its rising in the east. Fourthly, they saw a star when they left Jerusalem after Herod told them where the Child could be found.

Bethlehem was six miles from Jerusalem. The journey would take two and a half hours. As they travelled to Bethlehem on the final leg of their pilgrimage they looked and saw a star. The Scriptures say that the star which they saw in the east went before them. This is the first mention of the moving star. The fact is that a natural star like the one they saw in the east nearly two years earlier would not have remained in the heavens that period of time without being observed and documented by other astrologers.

The star in the east was the birth star of Jesus, whereas, the star which the wise-men observed while on their way to Bethlehem was the Bethlehem Star. The birth star was a natural body, while the Bethlehem star appears to be a supernatural event. The star guided the wise-men on the final six miles of their pilgrimage. It was without a doubt supernatural in nature; however, it appeared natural to the astrologers. The purpose of the star was to guide the wise-men to the house where Jesus resided. It operated like a global positioning system (GPS).

A supernatural light shined from above, and close to the ground ahead of the wise men as they travelled to Bethlehem. The light appeared to them as if it were coming from the tail of the star. The star stopped over the house where the young child Jesus lived.

Observe that the Bethlehem star displayed knowledge and intelligence. It knew where Jesus was staying. The star went before the astrologers, and directed them to the correct house where Jesus was living.

The characteristics of the Bethlehem star were contrary to those of the natural luminous heavenly bodies. That star was most likely directed by the supernatural. The Scriptures point to its supernatural elements saying, that "It came and stood over where the young Child was". Matthew 2:9.

The wise men entered the house where Joseph and Mary lived, and saw the young child with His mother. Jesus was born in June 10BCE according to the astrologist's calculations. Jesus was therefore two years old when the wise-men saw Him at Bethlehem.

The men went down on their knees at the feet of the Child Jesus, and worshipped Him. After they worshipped, they presented their gifts. They gave Him large quantities of gold, frankincense, and myrrh.

The gifts were a God-sent to the family. Joseph was experiencing some challenging financial times, and the gifts came at the right time.

The Wise Men

They were certainly well appreciated by Joseph. The Lord provided enough money for Joseph and Mary to adequately take care of his Son, Jesus.

After the wise-men completed their worship, and offered kind words to the family, they went on their way. They booked into the Bethlehem inn for rest and refreshments after the long journey.

The wisemen stayed at the inn for the night. That night, the Lord appeared to them in a dream and warned them not to return by way of Jerusalem nor report to Herod. They heeded the warning of the dream, and departed for their country, bypassing Jerusalem, so as to avoid King Herod. They went down in history as the first ambassadors to visit Jesus Messiah, King of the Jews. With mission accomplished, the wisemen went back to Susa rejoicing.

Joseph also got a dream soon after the wisemen departed Bethlehem. The angel of the Lord appeared to him, and told him to flee to Egypt, because Herod will be searching for Jesus to destroy Him. Joseph awoke from sleep and immediately made arrangements to leave Bethlehem, along with other Davidic descendants. Joseph quietly took his family to Alexandra in Egypt where many Jews lived.

The wisemen did not return to Herod. Now, Herod had no way of knowing the where-abouts of the child King. Herod was furious. In a rage, he sent a battalion of his soldiers to Bethlehem, and the coasts of Judea. Their order was to search and destroy all children aged two and under. They entered all the houses, pulling young children from their mother's arms. Killing them in their mother's presence.

The soldiers were merciless. They killed every young child they found. Mothers were weeping helplessly everywhere in Bethlehem and the coasts. See Matthew 2:16-18. But Jesus escaped because Joseph heeded the warning from the Lord. Joseph was already long gone, and on his way to Egypt when the massacre of the innocent children took place.

Chapter 13

What is Christmas?

Christmas is the celebration of the festival of the Nativity of Jesus. Scriptures declare Jesus Christ is the Lord of Glory, the One from eternity. Jesus Christ who in the form of God, and Lord of Heaven sets aside His glory, and came to Earth in the likeness of man. Christmas marks the day when God sent His only begotten Son into the world to save mankind.

The celebration of Christmas began in the 4th century. Up until that time, the main celebration of the church was the Easter celebration. There were many winter festivities in Europe, but none was sponsored by the church.

In Rome, the national celebration centered on Saturn, the Roman god. The pagan celebration called Saturnalia was observed in a hedonistic manner from the week before the winter solstice, December 21st, until two weeks into the New Year.

In the early years of the 4th century, Emperor Constantine was converted to Christianity. He adopted Christianity as the religion of the Roman Empire. He then became head of the Roman Imperial Church, and patron of the Christian faith.

Subsequently, Constantine discouraged pagan idolatry in the Roman Empire. Saturn was a Roman deity and the god of agriculture, after whom the winter festival Saturnalia was named. Since the state no longer approved of the god Saturn, the festival of Saturnalia became unpopular.

As a result of Saturnalia being out of favor with the emperor, the Church decided to create a national religious festival to replace that popular winter festival. Under the leadership of Pope Julius I, the Bishop of Rome, who ruled from 337CE to 352CE, the church instituted a festival called the "Feast of the Nativity", choosing the midpoint of the Roman winter celebration for the new religious church festivity. The date selected for the annual celebration was December 25th.

The nature of the religious feast quickly changed. Christianity replaced pagan deities as the state's religion; consequently, large numbers of ex-pagan worshippers joined the new religion. Most of the new members were not ready for the change to the Christian faith. Many were influential, unreformed by the new faith, and held on to their heathen ways of worship.

In an effort to accommodate the new adherents, the Church compromised its Christian values and adopted some of the pagan practices. Statues of their heathen gods were denounced by church leaders. However, to appease the newcomers the church installed images of the early Christian fathers in the church as replacement images.

Therefore, instead of statues of the gods Saturn, Jupiter, and Venus, the newcomers were introduced to statues of the saints: Peter, Paul, and Mary. The church also adopted other pagan elements of worship as practiced by the Romans. For example, incense burning was introduced during worship services, and the adoration and worship of images and statues were adopted by the church.

The Church festivity of the Nativity replaced the pagan festivity of Saturnalia. But then the Church adopted some of the pagan practices, and hedonism of Saturnalia, and incorporated them into the Nativity festival. The Nativity festival then became a mix of Christianity, hedonism, and secular events. The name of the festival was later changed to Christmas, but the religious, cultural, and secular elements remain to this day.

The celebration of Christmas Day on December 25th has been ingrained in the nations for centuries. That annual festivity is controlled by the world of commerce and will remain in the hands of the materialistic generation.

Christmas is more than a birthday party for Mary's first-born son Jesus. It is one of the most significant events in the history of humanity. The birthday of Jesus is a holy and sacred day. It was the day when the Holy One from eternity came to Earth and tabernacled in the flesh, and dwelt among men. Unfortunately, in today's world Christmas has lost its religious meaning.

The dominant secular nature, and the hedonistic flavor of the December 25th winter celebration called Christmas no longer truly represent the birthday of Jesus, the Son of God. Nevertheless, December 25th is far from being the real birthday of Jesus. According to Biblical records, the Virgin Mary conceived when Elizabeth was in the sixth month of pregnancy. Elizabeth got pregnant in Iylar/April. Therefore, Mary conceived in Tishri/ September. Based on a nine-month gestational period, it would appear that Jesus was born in the month of June. However, Pope Julius 1st, Bishop of Rome, arbitrarily selected December 25th to celebrate the Feast of the Nativity, which was renamed Christmas.

Chapter 14: Concept of Incarnation

There is a universal belief that sentient elements of the immaterial world exist. These supernatural elements are invisible having neither form nor shape. They are simply called spirits. Spirits are known to invade the natural world, and mingle with people. Some spirits have the ability to invade the body of humans or animals.

There are times when dominant spirits forcefully enter into the body of individuals. The embodied person will then possess two spirits. He will have his human spirit also called the mind, and that of the invading spirit. The incursive spirit is usually demonic, and more powerful than the human spirit. The demonic spirit will overpower the human spirit. The person will then lose control of his mind, and become the material representation of the invading demonic spirit.

The object of the demonic spirit is to take control of the persons actions. In many instances, the victim becomes insane, and will do the will and the bidding of the invading spirit. People or animals that are possessed by demon spirits become insane, exhibit very strange behaviors, and do crazy things. In many cases, such people who are out of their minds, are usually committed to psychiatric institutions.

Possessed people are not uncommon in today's world. Many such people are found in everywhere. Many are under psychiatric care and live in mental institutions.

Several accounts of demon-possessed people are documented in the Scriptures. In ancient Israel, King Saul was possessed by an evil spirit, and tried to kill David.[56] The New Testament Scriptures recorded an account of demon possessed men from the city of Gadara, that lived among the tombs.[57] Demonic embodiment is real, and is a very common malady in today's world.

The embodiment of a spirit into a person is called incarnation. The word incarnation is derived from the Latin word "incarnate", which, in turn comes from a combination of the Latin prefix "in" which carries the same meaning in English, and the suffix "carno" which means flesh. Together they essentially mean "in flesh".

According to WordNet, the word incarnate is defined as: *"clothed or embodied in flesh,"* and also means *"clothed or embodied in human or bodily form".*

There is also the ecclesiastical Latin word 'incarnatus' which is derived from 'in-carnis', and means "made flesh". Observe that the words incarnate and incarnatus although sharing the similar root words do have different meanings. Incarnate means 'in-flesh' whereas incarnatus means 'made flesh'.

Subsequently, the noun incarnation when derived from incarnate, presents a different concept from when it is derived from incarnatus. Incarnation when derived from the word incarnate means embodied in flesh, or invested with flesh or bodily nature, and form, especially human nature. Furthermore, it means a person who embodies in the flesh a deity, spirit, or abstract of quality.

On the other hand, the ecclesiastical Latin word incarnatus presents a different concept. Notably, the noun incarnation when derived from the word incarnatus literally means that spirit is made flesh, or became flesh. The Latin word incarnatus is sometimes misused and misapplied, and is confused with the word incarnate.

Chapter 15 Doctrine of the Incarnation of Christ

The word incarnation is not found in the Christian Bible, however the idea of the union of the divine and humanity is implied in the holy texts. Thereby, the terminology can be appropriately applied to the first coming of Christ.

It is universally believed by Christian believers that Christ came into the world through the concept of incarnation. However, the manner by which Christ entered the world, the time and location of His arrival has been misapprehended by church leaders for centuries. The biblical truth of the occasion has eluded theologians for millenniums. Notwithstanding, Catholic bishops meeting at ecumenical councils have pronounced the doctrine of the Incarnation of Christ based on the consensus of their thoughts, instead of on scriptural truths.

The bishop's original presentation of the doctrine of the Incarnation of Christ in the Nicene Creed has a strong biblical foundation. Not so with the enhanced version as recorded in the revised Nicene Creed. Unfortunately, in the revised Nicene Creed, the bishops pronounced the doctrine in a manner which falls short of good scriptural exegesis.

The doctrine of the incarnation was developed as an outcome of the ruling of the bishops at the Nicaea Synod of 325CE. In that year, the first Ecumenical Council of the Church was held at Nicaea in Bithynia (present day Iznik in Turkey). The synod lasted from May 20 – June 19, 325CE. The purpose of the meeting was to deal with a Christology dispute between two bishops from Alexandria in Egypt. The debate regarding the divinity of Jesus Christ lasted for one month. In the end, the Council referencing the early apostolic teachings declared that the Father and the Son are of the same substance, and are co-eternal.

As a resolution to the divinity disputation, the Ecumenical Council of 325CE formulated the Nicene Creed, which included a statement about the Incarnation of Christ. Consequently, the Nicene Creed was made a part of the foundational doctrine of the Christian faith. The creed was to be used as a yardstick of correct belief. It was formulated so as to identify heresy or deviations from the church interpretation of Biblical doctrines, as well as a confession of faith.

The Nicene Creed was based on the Apostles' teachings, but strong extra-biblical words were added to emphasize the relationship of Christ to the Father. The Greek word "homousis" was used to indicate that the Father and the Son were of one substance, and the Latin word 'incarnate' was used to articulate that Christ became man.

Nicene Creed

The Nicene Creed was drafted and presented to the Ecumenical Council of 325CE in the following manner:

> *We believe in one God, the Father Almighty, Maker of all things visible and invisible. And in one Lord Jesus Christ, the Son of God, begotten of the Father, that is, of the substance of the Father, God of God, light of light, true God of true God, begotten not made, of the same substance with the Father, through whom all things were made both in heaven and on earth; who for us men and our salvation descended, was incarnated, and was made man, suffered and rose again the third day, ascended into heaven and cometh to judge the living and the dead. And in the Holy Ghost.*

Doctrine of the Incarnation of Christ

The incarnation of Christ as stated in the creed set forth the foundational belief that God, the Logos (Word), assumed human form, and human nature (the fundamental disposition and traits of humans) in a hypostatic union. A hypostatic union is said to be the meeting of the Divine nature and the human nature in the person of Jesus Christ, who is both God and man. The Incarnation of Christ is essentially the union of divinity with humanity in the person of Jesus of Nazareth, who became the material representation of God on Earth.

The doctrine of the Incarnation is the very heart of Christianity, and is accepted by the estimated 2.6 billion Christians globally. They include Roman Catholics, Eastern Orthodox, Anglicans, Oriental Orthodox, Methodists, Assyrian Church of the East, Lutherans and Calvinists and Protestant denominations. The Nicene Creed is recited regularly in the liturgy of these churches as affirmation of their faith.

Revised Nicene Creed

The Incarnation of Christ is a foundational belief of the Christian church. Yet, the nature of the incarnation is partially misunderstood, and is mischaracterized by many church organizations.

The Nicene Creed was revised in 381CE by the Catholic bishops at the Constantinople Synod. The bishops determined that the original creed did not express the manner by which the Word (God)(Christ) was incarnated. They surmised that the incarnation took place instantaneously with the conception of the Virgin Mary.

Subsequently, the bishops argued that they found it necessary to revise the original text of 325CE, so as to strengthen the statement of faith, by interjecting a participating role for Mary, in the Incarnation of Christ.

The bishops were then tasked to make changes to the creed so as to reflect the way by which Christ came based on their interpretation. They did so by amending the creed in part, and adding a statement saying: "Christ came down from heaven, and was incarnate by the Holy Ghost, of the Virgin Mary, and was made man".

The modification of the creed actually meant that Christ was incarnate in Mary, that is to say: Christ was embodied in the Virgin Mary by the Holy Ghost. However, that is certainly not true. Another way the bishops expressed the idea was by using the ecclesiastical word 'incarnatus, which is past participle of 'incarni', meaning 'made flesh' or 'became flesh'.

By substituting the word incarnate of the original creed for incarnatus (made into flesh), the bishops changed the entire concept of the creed. The creed then read "Christ came down from heaven and incarnatus of the Virgin Mary of the Holy Ghost and was made man"; that is to say, Christ was made flesh or became flesh in the Virgin Mary.

The bishops changed the character of the creed by pronouncing that Christ was made flesh, yet they kept the word 'incarnate' which carries the meaning of 'appearing in flesh'. Therefore, the changes to the creed become rather muffled, in that the text echoes the meaning of the word incarnatus, yet the bishops switched and incorrectly used the word incarnate.

The amendment to the creed strongly implies that Christ was in Mary's womb with Jesus, for the duration of the gestation period of two hundred and eighty days. However, the claim that Christ was made flesh in Mary's womb is not supported by Scriptures. Nonetheless, this revised version was accepted by the Ecumenical Council of 381CE, and was pronounced the doctrinal statement of true belief.

Thus, as many as 99% of the estimated 2.6 billion Catholics and Christians erroneously believe the Catholic pronouncement, that the Incarnation of Christ took place simultaneously with the conception of the Virgin Mary.

Chapter 16
Religious Malpractice

The 381CE revised Nicene Creed asserts that Christ came down from Heaven, and was incarnated in Mary by the Holy Spirit. This statement is merely a hypothesis. The idea that Christ was incarnated in Mary is not recorded in the holy Scriptures. Furthermore, that erroneous assertion leads to the rather unsubstantiated claim that Christ was in Mary's womb during the gestation period of nine months.

Such outlandish ideas are foreign to the Scriptures. Yet, this is the precise message that the bishops of the First Constantinople Ecumenical Council of 381CE wanted to convey, when they added words to the original Nicene Creed. Apparently, the bishops wanted to give the impression that Mary was the mother of Christ (God).

Unfortunately, the notion that Christ was incarnated in Mary is derived from the text of John 1:14. Here it is recorded that the Word was made flesh. And the ecclesiastical word incarnatus aligned perfectly with that text.

John 1:14, therefore, seems to be a sound scriptural foundation for the doctrine of the Incarnation of Christ. The text clearly shows that divinity and humanity unite in one person, namely Jesus Christ. The Catholic bishops then asserted that Christ was made flesh in the womb of the Virgin Mary, and that Christ was with the holy seed in Mary's womb from the time of her conception. However, this is mere speculation since there is no scriptural proof.

Possible Error in Translation

The words of the text of John 1:14 which states that "the Word (God) was made flesh" poses a problem. Firstly, the words 'made flesh' carries the connotation that the Word (God) was created. This is far from the truth. The fact is this: God creates all things, and any suggestion that God the Creator made Himself into flesh is absurd.

Secondly, the "Word" in the text is a direct reference to Jesus Christ, Son of God. The Scriptures state that Jesus, the Son of God was begotten, and not made. Jesus was born and not created. Scriptures reveal Him as the only begotten Son of God.[58]

The truth is this; all things that exist were created, except God. Therefore, Jesus Christ, the Son of God, and God the Son was not made (created). The Scriptures expressly state that God was manifest in the flesh. That is, He appeared in human form.[59] Since it can be proven that the Word was not converted into flesh, then the wording of the text of John 1:14 is strongly suggestive of an error.

The original words of the Scriptures are oracles of God. There is no suggestion of inerrancy in the original Scriptures because every scripture is God-breathed, and was given by divine inspiration. So then, God is the author of His perfect word.[60] The original manuscripts of the Scriptures are authentic and are therefore the true word from God. We also know that scripture does not contradict scripture; instead, Scriptures complement one another.

However, man is imperfect and is prone to errors. Mistakes in both the translation and the interpretation of the Scriptures are therefore possible, and did occur in some instances. With this in mind, a close look at the text of John 1:14 compared to other Scriptures will highlight possible translational errors.

Detailed examination of the passage indicates that John's original manuscript may have been copied. It is therefore possible that the passage of John 1:14 was incorrectly transcribed, or an error was made when the text was translated from Greek into Latin.

The possibility of translation errors was stated by Reverend George Mastrantonis of the Greek Orthodox Church of American his article, "The Bible: Its Original Language and English Translations". Reverend Mastrantonis in his in-depth article on Bible translations wrote that some of the English versions of the New Testament were made from Greek manuscripts that contained many mistakes. Those faulty Greek manuscripts were most likely due to poor transcription.

Very likely, all translations from the possible erroneously transcribed Greek manuscripts perpetuated the error that the Word was made flesh. This can be proven in John's later writings of his epistles, where no mention was made that God was made into flesh or became flesh. John instead emphasized that Christ came in the flesh, meaning that He was manifested in human form.

John recorded that Christ came in the flesh in two separate passages. First, he wrote to the Church to teach the believers how to recognize the Spirit of God working in individuals. He said: "Hereby know ye (recognize) the Spirit of God: Every spirit that confesseth that *Jesus Christ is come in the flesh* is of God".[61] Again in 2nd John 1:7, the apostle declared that *"Jesus Christ is come in the flesh"*.

The term "come in the flesh" means to appear in human form. It certainly does not carry the same meaning as 'made flesh' or 'became flesh', meaning that God the Spirit became material flesh. Those two passages in 1st John also contradict the hypophysis that the Word was made flesh. It is quite obvious that one of those statements is incorrect. If the truth is settled at the mouth of two witnesses, then the two passages of 1st John 4:2-3 and 2 John 1:7 settles the matter that the Spirit of God (Christ) was not made flesh, but that He was clothed in the flesh.

There is another text of the Scriptures that indirectly refutes the idea that the Word (Christ) was made flesh. Paul wrote that God was manifest in the flesh.[62] Here Paul emphasized that God was not made flesh, but he appeared in the flesh, that is in human flesh and clothed in humanity.

A Correct Interpretation

There is one Bible translation that renders the passage of John 1:14 in the correct manner. That translation is the 1904 edition of the "Weymouth New Testament". That translation of John 1: 14 reads: "And the Word came in the flesh, and lived for a time in our midst, so that we saw His glory—the glory as of the Father's only Son, sent from His presence. He was full of grace and truth."[63]

The Weymouth translation affirms that God was manifested in human form, but did not say how, when or where the incarnation occurred. The biblical truth is that God is Spirit. The spirit nature and the flesh nature are separate and distinct, and are governed by the law of God. Flesh cannot become spirit, neither can Spirit become flesh.

However, spirit can be linked with the flesh, but they cannot blend together or synthesis as one inseparable unit. Jesus confirmed this law when He said that flesh is flesh and spirit is spirit. Flesh gives birth to flesh and Spirit gives birth to spirit.[64] God can do all things, but God is immutable and will not violate His divine laws.

Flesh will remain flesh, and spirit will remain spirit. Flesh nature is of a lower value and cannot give birth to the spirit nature which is of a higher value. The Virgin Mary is flesh, and could not give birth to Christ who is Spirit.

Therefore, according to God's law of natures, the Word (God) cannot be made into flesh. However, Spirit can enter into, and embody the flesh, and the two natures can co-exist in one person. In this case the Incarnation of Christ as indicated in John 1:14 could read thus: "The Word came in the flesh". The Catholic pronouncement that Christ came down from Heaven and was incarnate (made flesh) in Mary is not supported by Scriptures and is without merit.

Chapter 17
The Catholic Hypothesis

Catholics assert that God became flesh in the Virgin Mary. This hypothesis is written in the revised Nicene Creed. The creed was revised in 381CE. It states in part that Christ came down from Heaven, and was incarnate by the Holy Ghost of the Virgin Mary, and was made man. The inference here is that Christ became flesh in the womb of the Virgin Mary.

Revised Nicene Creed

The revised creed states: We believe in one God, the Father Almighty, Maker *of heaven and earth*, and of all things visible and invisible. And in one Lord Jesus Christ, the *only-begotten* Son of God, **begotten of the Father before all worlds (aeons),** Light of Light, very God of very God, begotten, not made, being of one substance with the Father; by whom all things were made; who for us men, and for our salvation, came down from heaven, and was **incarnate** ***by the Holy Ghost of the Virgin Mary,*** and was **made** man; *He was crucified for us under Pontius Pilate,* and suffered, *and was buried,* and the third day He rose again, *according to the Scriptures, and* ascended into heaven, *and sitteth on the right hand of the Father;* from thence He shall come again, *with glory,* to judge the quick and the dead; *whose kingdom shall have no end.* And in the Holy Ghost, *the Lord and giver of life, who proceedeth from the Father, who with the Father and the Son together is worshipped and glorified, who spake by the prophets. In one holy catholic and apostolic Church; we acknowledge one baptism for the remission of sins; we look for the resurrection of the dead, and the life of the world to come. Amen.*[65]

The bishops at the Ecumenical Council of Ephesus in 431CE reasoned that since Christ was incarnated in Mary, and gave birth to Jesus, and since Jesus is God, then Mary gave birth to God. The bishops then used the Greek word 'theotokia', which means God-bearer, to define Mary. Accordingly, they pronounced the title of 'Mother of God' on Mary.

The bishops also claim that the 'Mother of God' title was to affirm the central truth of the Incarnation of Christ. However, there is no scripture that indicate that Christ was incarnated in Mary or that Mary gave birth to Christ, or that she was the mother of God.

The peculiar Catholic ruling that Mary is the mother of God allowed the Church to elevate Mary to a position above that of humans. Consequently, the Catholic church and her adherents exalt Mary to the unbiblical position of 'mother of God'. Thereby, Catholics erroneously add Mary to the Triune Godhead.

Furthermore, they took divinity, and honor and glory which belongs to God, and gave it to a human. Be it known that God does not share. Therefore, such an act of adding Mary to the Holy Trinity is an act of blasphemy.

Unfortunately, Catholic teachers deceive millions of Christians with false teachings, that the Virgin Mary is the mother of God, and cause them to recite prayers to Mary. Thereby, the Catholic faithful unknowingly partakes in the sin of blasphemy, and idolatry by accepting that Mary has a share in God's work of salvation, and worshipping her.

Catholic theology relating to the nativity of Jesus seems to be way out of alignment with the word of God. Their dogmas relating to the Incarnation of Christ and the Virgin Mary are false, and shows either a lack of understanding, or willful ignorance of the Scriptures.

A knowledge of the nature and character of God would be helpful to understand the profound mystery of God and the Incarnation of

The Catholic Hypothesis

Christ. The Bible reveals that God is a Supreme Being who is from everlasting, and that he existed before all things. Furthermore, the Scripture declares God to be self-existent, and is the possessor and giver of life.

God inhabits eternity, and rules the universe from His throne in Heaven. God is the all-sufficient supernatural Being who is beyond all limits of time and space. He is without a beginning, and has within Him the power to cause things to come into being. Thereby, God is the qualified creator of the universe and of man.[66]

God is a Spirit.[67] He is immortal, invisible, omniscient, omnipotent, omnipresent, immutable, and is King Eternal. God is Lord, and possesses all power and authority over His creation.

God is a mystery which man cannot solve. Man's knowledge of God is limited to the revelations in the Scriptures, and also through visions. Many people both Christians and Jews in this generation, and in the days of the apostles, could not comprehend the mystery of God.

Catholics assertion that God became flesh in Mary's womb is therefore absurd. It is illogical to think that the Supreme Eternal God who created all things was then birthed by one of his creatures.

It is rather outrageous for Bible scholars or church leaders or for anyone to utter the words that Creator God or Christ was in the womb of Mary for nine months, and that she gave birth to God. Such assertions insult, and demean the holy God, by diminishing his stature and greatness and reducing him to a creature of the womb. Such travesty is the essence of blasphemy.

The postulation that Mary is the mother of God, no doubt comes from the erroneously translated or transcribed text of John 1:14 which says that "the Word was made flesh". However, the Scriptures proved that the 'Word (God)' who has no beginning, and no end was not made flesh, neither was Christ birthed. These infallible truths are recorded in the Bible, and available to all, and so man has no excuse for their transgressions.

Chapter 18

Never in the Womb

The Catholic Church got the Incarnation of Christ all wrong. The truth is this, two thousand and thirty years ago, God came into the material world, and appeared in human form in the person of Jesus Christ. However, the baseless claims that Christ was incarnated at the time of the conception of Mary, and that Mary gave birth to Christ (God), are proven false by the Scriptures.

The Catholic's assertion that Christ was incarnated by the Holy Ghost in Mary, at the time of her conception is pure speculation. The fact is that conception occurs at the time when the egg is fertilized. However, Mary's conception was unlike any other.

Whereas incarnation means embodiment; the assertion that Christ embodied the microscopic seed (holy thing) is illogical. Yet, the prevailing universal concept of the doctrine of the Incarnation of Christ is that God (Spirit) became flesh at the moment of conception of the Virgin Mary. However, that idea is not scriptural, and is merely a conjecture.

The truth is that the Scriptures prove beyond the shadow of a doubt that Christ was never in Mary's womb. Therefore, Mary never gave birth to God or Christ. Unfortunately, more than a billion Catholics and millions of Christians of other faith, earnestly believe the false narrative that Christ was in Mary, and that she birthed Him.

The first proof that Jesus Christ was not in Mary's womb is given by the Angel Gabriel. Luke stated that the angel Gabriel was sent by

God to Nazareth. The angel told Mary that she was chosen by God to bear the holy seed. This was the seed of the woman which God promised that would crush the head of the serpent.

It seems worthwhile therefore, to relate the Gabriel's story of the conception of Mary. The angel told Mary that the Holy Ghost will overshadow her, and she shall conceive, and the holy thing which shall be born of her shall be called the Son of God.[68]

Observe two important things that the angel said. Firstly, he referred to the unborn (fetus) not as a person, nor as a deity, nor as Christ. He called it a holy thing. Be cognizant of the fact that the angel Gabriel stands in the presence of God. He is a messenger of God. Gabriel would not dare call the holy God a 'holy thing'. The holy thing was not deity. It was a fertilized egg (seed) that the Holy Spirit placed in Mary's womb. It was holy because it came from heaven, and it was pure and undefiled, and had no trace of Adam's blood, therefore it was untainted by sin.

The holy thing (seed) was material in nature. It was a natural substance. The truth is this; God is Spirit, likewise Christ is of the same substance. Therefore, the holy thing was not God or Christ. Moreover, if it was deity the angel who ministers in the presence of God, would not refer to it as a thing.

The holy thing in Mary's womb was the body that was being prepared to receive Christ. The writer of the book of Hebrews made this abundantly clear when he wrote that a body was prepared, and made ready for Christ before He came into the world. The divine principle of creation and procreation is that the natural body comes first and after that the spiritual. See 1st Corinthians 15:46.

The author wrote: Hence, when He (Christ) entered into the world, He said, "Sacrifices and offerings You {God} have not desired, but instead You {God} have made ready a body for me [to offer]."[69] That prepared body was birthed as a male-child. Christ therefore did not come while the body was developing in Mary's womb.

Secondly, the angel did not ascribe deity to the holy thing. Therefore, it was not Christ. Gabriel told Mary that at birth the status of the holy thing will change. At birth it will be no more a thing, but it will be a person; and shall be called the Son of God. So then, the holy thing was the developing physical body of Jesus. The fetus (holy thing) in Mary's womb was natural. It was void of the Spirit, because natural body can only produce natural body.

The prophet Isaiah foretold that the virgin would give birth to a child, and after that, God gave the Son. So then, the son was not birthed, but was given. Isaiah wrote: "For unto us a child is born, unto us a son is given…"[70]

Moreover, the prophet Micah prophesied that 'the Ancient of Days', who is God will come to Bethlehem, and a be Ruler. Observe that Mary conceived in Nazareth, but gave birth at Bethlehem.

The Scriptures say that King Herod demanded that the chief priests and scribes tell him the place where Christ will be born. They told him that Christ would be born in Bethlehem, according to the prophet Micah.

According to the Scriptures, at that very moment of delivery, the Lord came from eternity (Micah 5:2) and embodied the new-born baby. Hereby, Scriptures show that Christ was in eternity while the holy thing was in Mary's womb.

Here we see a process. First comes the natural (physical) body, and after birth take place then comes the spiritual. This was the principle from the beginning of creation. See 1st Corinthians 15:46, Genesis 2:7.

Here we are presented with credible witnesses against the idea that Christ was in Mary's womb. From the Scriptures comes one Apostle of Jesus Christ, two prophets, and the angel Gabriel, who stands in the presence of God. All four witnesses presented evidences that completely dismiss the idea of an intrauterine Christ.

Chapter 19 How God Became Man

The manifestation of God in human form is a great mystery. Many Christians in this generation do not understand how God became a man. Likewise, many Jews cast doubt on the mystery of how God was revealed in human flesh. But true Christians operate in the realm of faith and believe the word of God as it is written.

True believers therefore have an unshakeable belief that Jesus Christ is the Son of God. They believe that He lived among men on earth, and that He died for the sin of the world. On the other hand, Jews demand substantial, and scriptural proof of God's mode of entry into the natural world. They want to know how the invisible God appeared in human form. These are reasonable questions.

The Bible said a lot about the coming of the Messiah into time and space. God will not have us to be ignorant concerning spiritual things. Therefore, He provided all relevant information in the Scriptures. The prophets of old announced His first coming in many passages of Scriptures.

About 750BCE the prophet Isaiah gave a sign from God regarding the coming of the Lord in human form. Isaiah prophesied that a virgin shall conceive and bear a son, and shall call his name Immanuel. The name Immanuel mean 'God with us'. See Isaiah 7:14.

The appointed time came, and God selected a young woman named Mary as the chosen vessel to bear the holy seed. Mary was engaged to a young man named Joseph. They were both direct descendants of King David.

The Bible records that while Mary was at Nazareth God sent the angel Gabriel to deliver a message to her. Gabriel told Mary that she found favor with God, and she shall conceive and have a son. She should name him Jesus. Moreover, he shall be called the Son of the Highest.[71]

The angel further informed Mary as to how she shall conceive. Gabriel told her: "The Holy Ghost shall come upon thee the power of the Highest shall overshadow thee: therefore, also that holy thing which shall be born of thee shall be called the Son of God". Luke 1:35.

Then soon after the angel departed from her, the Holy Spirit came and overshadowed her. He miraculously placed the holy seed in Mary's womb, and she conceived and became pregnant.

The holy seed grew, and formed the physical body of Jesus. The holy thing (fetus) in Mary's womb was completely isolated. The unborn child had no physical or physiological contact with Mary. However, it had indirect contact by means of the umbilical cord. The cord was attached to the placenta which is connected to Mary. Thereby the developing fetus received nourishment from Mary by the process of osmosis.

At the time when Mary was in her third trimester, and was about seven months pregnant, she travelled with her husband Joseph to Bethlehem. They were forced to go to their ancestral homeland to register for the Roman census. They left Nazareth in the early Spring at the end of March 10BCE. They travelled by way of the Jordan Valley, and up to Jerusalem.

The young pregnant Mary travelled the entire distance by foot. It was a grueling journey. The road was dusty and rough. She traversed deep valleys and up the mountains. The journey took eight days and they arrived in Jerusalem in time for the Feast of the Passover. The Passover that year began on Monday, the 15th of April, 10BCE. The couple stayed in Jerusalem and participated in the holy festival. At the end of the Passover celebration, they continued on to Bethlehem, the city of David.

Mary and Joseph arrived in Bethlehem after a long and arduous journey. The trip took a total of about twelve days, including the stopover in Jerusalem. Mary was exhausted. In her state of advanced pregnancy, she needed a place to relax comfortable.

Joseph searched all over Bethlehem for lodging, but could not find any apartment to rent. The young couple became anxious. Joseph never gave up. He now resolves that he would take any place that has a roof. He kept on searching. Finally, he found a cave on the outskirts of Bethlehem. Joseph was so desperate; he had no choice but to take possession of the cave. He then used his carpentry skills to make it into a habitable place. The young couple moved into their humble cave-home, and lived there for some time.

The Scriptures state that while they were living in Bethlehem, the time came for Mary to deliver her first-born child. See Luke 2:6-7. Mary was relaxing in her humble cave-home enjoying the balmy late Spring weather. Suddenly, she started having contractions. She knew that the time has arrived for her to give birth.

Joseph desired that his wife give birth in the comfort of the inn. He rushed into town and tried to book a room. He had no luck. The inn-keeper told him that there was no private room available. Disappointed, he went back to his cave-home. Joseph hurriedly went and called the midwife. Mary had no choice but to deliver her baby in the cave-home.

The midwife came in the late evening hours. She immediately got to work. The baby came forth from the womb in a normal way, and without any problems. Mary's first-born son was the holy human body that was prepared in the Virgin Mary to receive the Spirit of Christ.

God is Spirit and has neither form nor shape. Christ therefore required a natural body so as to come into the material world as a man. He needed the physical body as a requirement of the Redeemer. A body of a man to be sacrificed for the sins of the world. A human body to shed its blood and die in the place of man to satisfy Divine justice.

The writer of the book of Hebrews wrote concerning the body of Christ saying: "Hence, when He (Christ) entered into the world, He said, Sacrifices and offerings You have not desired, but instead You have made ready a body for Me (to offer). In burnt offerings and sin offerings You have taken no delight. Then said I, Lo, here I am come to do your will O God; to fulfill what is written of Me in the volume of the Book". Hebrews 10: 5-7 AMP., Psalm 40:6-8

At the moment of birth, when Mary's first boy-child was separated from the womb, God activated the divine spiritual pathway for Christ to enter into the material world. In an instant, and unseen by Mary and her attendants; the invisible pre-existing God; the One from eternity who has no beginning, and no end, came to Bethlehem to the delivery room.

Then, in a twinkling of an eye a great miracle took place. Immediately as the baby exited the womb, the Spirit of God entered Mary's first-born son, as He took His first breath.[72]

Christ came into the world by the ordained principle whereby the physical body comes first, and then the spiritual. See 1st Corinthians 15:46. This was the same principle that God used in the beginning when he created Adam. It is also the same principle that he uses for every human being. He gives the human spirit at birth when the baby is separated from the womb.

Mary's new-born child was holy, sinless and undefiled. He was a new creation. Mary's child was the second Adam. However, Jesus did not get a created human spirit. Instead, He received a full measure of the Spirit of God.

So then, by the act of God, Divinity united with humanity. The amazing mystery of how God became Man was revealed when the Spirit of God embodied Mary's new-born son, Jesus.

At the time of His birth in Bethlehem, the embodying Spirit instantly gave Jesus His divine nature, and the Son of God became God the Son. The divine nature was united with human nature in the person of Jesus. In essence, Jesus received the full measure of the Spirit of God,[73] therefore, He is of the same substance as God the Father.

Thus, Jesus was fully God and fully man. He then became the material representation of God on earth. It is noteworthy that Christ received the title of Son of God at the time of the birth of Mary's first-born son, but that was not the beginning of Christ.

Christ is Spirit who has no beginning. He was not born that day, and absolutely, never was born. However, the material body which was the holy tabernacle of the Spirit of Christ came forth from the womb of Mary. The natural baby was embodied by the Spirit at birth, was called the Son of God and named Jesus. Nevertheless, the day when Mary gave birth in Bethlehem is regarded as the birthday of Jesus. Christ is Lord, and the Lord God has no beginning. Therefore, prior to that day and throughout eternity He existed as God the Holy Spirit.

The prophet Isaiah prophesied about the coming of God into time and space saying: "Unto us a child is born, (indicating humanity) unto us a son (indicating deity) is given: and his name shall be called Wonderful, Counsellor, The Mighty God, The Everlasting Father, The Prince of Peace."[74]

The prophet showed that the Son that was given was of the same substance as the Father; and gave Him identical titles, suggesting that the Father and the Son are One. Jesus affirmed that truth when He declared in a homily in the Temple that "I and My Father are one".[75] His affirmation of deity infuriated the Jews and they took stones to stone Him, because He makes Himself equal with God. See John 10:30-31.

Here then is a great mystery of God. There is God the Father, "God the Son – Christ", and God the Holy Spirit, seemingly separate deities, yet they are One by the Spirit. The oneness of God is declared in Scriptures. "Hear O Israel: The Lord our God is one Lord."[76] God is a great mystery which no one can comprehend.

The Apostle Paul wrote concerning the mystery of God, saying: "Beyond all questions, the mystery of godliness is great: He appeared in a body, was vindicated by the Spirit, was seen by angels, was preached among the nations, was believed on in the world, was taken up in glory."[77]

Micah's prophecy is biblical proof that Christ came into the world at the time of the birth of Mary's first-born son. He did not come at the time of her conception, nor when the holy thing was in her womb, as Catholic theology erroneously asserts.

The truth is this. Mary conceived in Nazareth, and gave birth to a boy-child in Bethlehem, Judah. Then the Holy Spirit (the One from

Eternity/God) went to Bethlehem at the very moment when the child was born and immediately embodied Him.

The fact is that the embodiment (incarnation) of Christ took place after the baby was born. This proves beyond the shadow of a doubt that Christ was never in Mary's womb. It must therefore be strongly emphasized that the Virgin Mary did not give birth to Christ or to God. The Roman Catholic's absurd assertion that Mary gave birth to Christ, and that she is mother of God is false, and unscriptural, and is pure conjecture.

Chapter 20 False Doctrines

All Christian churches have core religious beliefs that they hold and teach. Such beliefs are usually grounded in the Scriptures. However, those beliefs are subject to the church's interpretations of the word of God. There are also many church doctrines and dogmas that are based upon tradition.

Nevertheless, the only true doctrines are those that are based upon the correct interpretation of Scriptures. With that in mind, we will examine some of the dogmas that are spawned from the doctrine of the Incarnation of Christ.

The doctrine of the Incarnation of Christ is the belief that God came to Earth and manifested himself in human form, in the person of Jesus Christ. There are no hidden mysteries in the divine embodiment of Jesus at the time of His birth. Yet, the Catholic Church, and other church denominations have for centuries taught that Christ became flesh in Mary's womb.

The bishops that drafted the Doctrine of the Incarnation of Christ at the Constantinople Ecumenical Council in 381CE, were highly educated theologians. They were great religious leaders, and devoted men, yet they misrepresented the way by which Christ came into the world. Seemingly, they lacked spiritual discernment and did not understand the mysteries of God. They are a good portrayal of Nicodemus who went to see Jesus by night.

A Divine Mystery

Nicodemus was a powerful Jewish religious leader at the time of Jesus. He knew the Scriptures, and was a keeper of the Law, but he was not born again. This means that he did not possess the indwelling presence of the Holy Spirit. Therefore, it is no surprise that he did not understand spiritual things because only the Spirit can reveal spiritual things. Simply put, Nicodemus was not born of the Spirit.

The Scriptures contain much information relating to the nativity of Jesus. However, the carnal mind cannot understand the things of God. Book knowledge is of great value, but only the spirit-filled believer can understand some of the deep secrets of the word of God.

It is therefore, not a surprise that the learned bishops failed to recognize the way by which Christ came into the material world. Obviously, they lack spiritual guidance. The Scriptures make it plain that God reveals spiritual things only to those that are saved.[78] Perhaps, the bishops were like the unsaved Nicodemus.

It appears that the bishops were spiritually blind, and lacked the capacity to understand the mystery of how Christ came into the material world. Subsequently, they resorted to the human intellect, and surmised incorrectly that Christ was incarnate in Mary. Unfortunately, this error left the door wide open for a spate of false ideas and dogmas to creep into the church.

The Catholic church often uses spurious dogmas to elevate the status and the teachings of the church. They pronounce many false doctrines relating to the Virgin Mary, which were defined by popes and theologians of the church.

The purpose of the dogmas was to express Catholic statements of belief. These are forced upon adherents, and faithful Catholics must observe them without question or objection. Moreover, the popes who pronounce the false dogmas claim infallibility thereby deceiving the laypeople and compelling them to accept the wine of false doctrines.

The Catholic bishops of the Ecumenical Council of Ephesus in 431CE improperly pronounced the Virgin Mary as the mother of God. Then, over the centuries, popes have defined the Marian doctrine of Divine Motherhood. Thereby, they erroneously teach that since Mary was the mother of Jesus, and since Jesus is Lord, then she is mother of God.

But such teaching is false, because the Scriptures document that God is from everlasting. God has no beginning, and no one existed before him, therefore he has no mother. Moreover, God is Spirit, and Mary who is flesh cannot give birth to Spirit. Also, it is impossible for the creature to give birth to the Creator.

It seems that the Catholic church use biased theological interpretations, and unsound doctrines to lead the church of an estimated billion people into the bypath religion of Mariology. Moreover, the Church went rogue with other spurious Marian doctrines that led millions of followers unwittingly down a bypath of idolatry.

The Catholic Church embrace the false doctrine of the Immaculate Conception. This dogma states that God preserved Mary from original sin at the time of her conception in her mother's womb. There is no scriptural foundation for that dogma. On the contrary, the Scriptures declare that people are sinful from the time their mother conceived them. Therefore, all humans are born as sinners.[79]

No descendant of Adam is exempt from the curse of sin, not even the Virgin Mary since the Bible declares that all have sinned.[80] Observe that the Law considered Mary a sinner. The Scriptures say that Mary took Jesus to the Temple on the day of her purification. The Law requires that she present two doves to the priest at the entrance of the Temple. One was sacrificed as a burnt offering, and the other was a sin offering for her, whereby, the priest made atonement for her.

The Virgin Mary was pure and innocent, but not without sin. She possessed original sin when the angel Gabriel visited her and at the time of conception. However, she believed God's message concerning the conception, and the birth of Jesus, the Son of God. Thus, due to her faith in the angel's message, she gained a right standing with God. Nonetheless, she was still burdened with the original sin, until Jesus died on the cross, and paid the price for man's redemption.

The dogma of the Immaculate Conception runs contrary to the expressed word of God. Yet the dogma is said to be a divinely revealed truth which must be accepted without questioning. This erroneous dogma was pronounced by Pope Pius IX in ineffabillis in 1854.[81]

The Catholic Church also pronounce the attribute of deity upon Mary. They teach the blasphemous doctrine of Redemptrix. This dogma falsely claim that Mary was taken up into Heaven where she is positioned in glory as an advocate, and a dispenser of grace. Moreover, the dogma asserts that Mary is given a share of God's divine work of salvation, in partnership with Jesus Christ. This sacrilegious dogma is foreign to the Scriptures and is offensive to God.

Mary's Perpetual Virginity is another spurious Catholic dogma that was defined by the pope. Hereby, the Catholic church presents Mary as a virgin before she was conceived, and for her entire life. This dogma is not biblical. The Scriptures record that Mary had several children after Jesus was born. Matthew wrote that Jesus had four brother and an unknown number of sisters. See Matthew 12:46, Mark 6:3.

After a long evangelical mission, Jesus returned to Nazareth where He grew up. He went into their synagogue and opened the scroll and taught from the Scriptures. The people remembered Him as a carpenter. They did not accept Him as a rabbi, and were offended by His teachings. They recognized Jesus as the son of Mary, and acknowledged His siblings. Then some of the people asked saying: "Is not this the carpenter's son? Is not His mother called Mary? And His brethren James, and Joses, and Simon, and Judas? And His sisters, are they not all with us?"[82]

These are recorded indisputable truths from the Scriptures, which prove that Mary had at least six children after Jesus was born. This is scriptural proof that Mary did not remain a virgin after she gave birth to Jesus. Therefore, the Catholic Dogma of Perpetual Virginity is without merit, and is a false doctrine.

Then there is the spurious doctrine of the Assumption. The Catholic infers that Mary had special privileges because she was completely free from sin, and also because of her immaculate conception. Therefore, they assert that at the end of her life on Earth she did not see decay of her body. Hence, Roman Catholic leaders presumptuously claim that by virtue of Mary's immaculate conception, God chose that she would be taken up body and soul into heaven to reign as queen.[83]

False Doctrines

There is not a hint of truth to the wild assertion that Mary's body was taken up into heaven. According to the Scriptures, all people who died will await the day of resurrection. Mary will also await that glorious day, which is yet to come. Neither is she promoted to the title of 'Queen of Heaven'. The truth is that there is no queen in Heaven. This is all the product of the imagination, and Catholic fiction.

The spiritual damage caused by false doctrines, due to possible willful ignorance of Catholic church leaders is quite evident today. Over the centuries, the Catholics built many churches in honor of the Virgin Mary. The church elevates Mary to the position of deity, and venerate her as a goddess, and adore her as the Queen of Heaven. They adorned her image with beautiful garments and crown her with gold.

The Catholic church even developed prayers to Mary, 'Mother of God', which according to the church, entrusts the petitions to Mary. Catholics are taught to pray to God through Mary. One such church prayer reads: "Holy Mary, Mother of God; pray for us sinners, now and at the hour of our death". Thereby, totally trusting in Mary, rather than in God.

Whereas the Lord God commands that no one should make images or statues or worship them. Yet, Catholics justify images of Mary, and other saints, and indulge in the ungodly practice of idolatrous worship. Multiple millions of Catholic believers around the world adore and worship images of the Virgin Mary.

The false doctrines of the Catholic Church cause millions of the faithful to practice idolatry. Many choose to worship by sight and not by faith, and willingly participate in idolatrous worship. Catholics claim that their act of bowing and prostrating themselves before images of Mary and other saints is a way to worship God whom they cannot see.

The truth is that nothing should come between God and the worshipper. If an image stands between the worshipper and God, then the worship is directed towards the image, and not to God. The Bible teaches that worship belongs to God only. All reverence, adoration, praise, veneration and exaltation should be given to God only. God does not share His glory and will not accept shared worship.

The Bible makes it plain in many passages that God should be the only object of worship. Jesus emphasized the truth when He rebuked the Devil, saying, "Thou shalt worship the Lord thy God and Him only shalt thou serve."[84] Unfortunately, many Christian believers lack knowledge of the Scriptures, and are therefore easily deceived by false teachers.

Millions of Catholic believers and other Christians are innocently drawn into, and participate in worship that venerates both God and saints and by doing so transgress the Law of God.

Today, over two billion Christians, mostly Catholics, believe the false teaching that Mary gave birth to Christ, and is therefore the mother of God. The false teachings are the result of poor biblical exegesis, and in some cases, willful ignorance. Church leaders usually make scriptural error because of misinterpretation of the Scriptures. Unfortunately, false teachings have shipwrecked the faith of millions of unsuspecting Christian believers from different denominations around the world.

The Apostle Paul prophesied of this day and time in history, when he said that in the last days there will be a great falling away from the faith, and believers would follow after false teachers in the church, and doctrines of demons.

Paul wrote: "The time will come when they (people) will not endure (accept) sound doctrine; but after their own lusts shall heap to themselves teachers, having itching ears; and they shall turn away their ears from the truth, and shall be turned unto fables."[85]

Chapter 21 — A Message to the Churches

The church is a universal body of Christian believers who have been called out from the world by God, to live righteously under the authority of Jesus Christ. The church was formed by the power of the Holy Spirit, on the Day of Pentecost, Sunday, May 23rd 30CE. There were one hundred and twenty men and women in the first assembly of worshippers. However, since its inception, the number of livings professing Christian believers have increased to an estimated 2.6 billion in the year 2020CE.

The purpose of the church is to love the Lord God, and to worship him in spirit and in truth, and to love our fellow-men as ourselves. While the divine mission of the church is to preach the Gospel of Jesus Christ to the nations. Evangelism, and saving souls are her primary goals.

The universal church is made up of thousands of local churches that fall under many Christian denominations. The adherents are people who acknowledge Jesus Christ as Lord, and Savior, and confess their sins, and ask God to forgive them of their trespasses.

The churches are not perfect religious institutions. The churches today, like the churches of the first century have many faults. Some churches compromised with pagans, some have corrupt teachers, some deceive believers into committing immorality, and some practice idolatry. Also, many become spiritually anemic, being weary, cold, and unresponsive to the moving of the Spirit.

The Lord is speaking to the churches in these last days, just as He spoke to the churches of the first century. The message is not one of condemnation but a message to awaken the church. A message to the church to recognize her shortcomings so that she can amend her ways. A message for her to return to her godly commissioned purpose and calling. This is a timely and urgent message, calling her to remove the spots from her garments, trim her lamps, and get ready to meet the bridegroom.

The Lord is speaking to the Catholic Church today. A church whose membership totals an estimated 1.34 billion adherents. This number is more than half of the total Christian population in the world today. The Lord loves the Catholic Church. Notwithstanding, the Scriptures declare that the Lord admonishes all those whom He loves. The writer of Hebrews wrote that: "The Lord corrects and disciplines everyone whom He loves, and He punishes, even scourges every son whom He accept, and welcomes to His heart, and cherishes."[86]

To the Catholic Church

The Catholic church has taken a bypath. She has negotiated a compromise with the pagan society. She believes that spiritual liberty gives her the leeway to practice idolatry. The utilization of idols and images of any kind is forbidden by the word of God. The Mariology dogmas are without scriptural foundations, and are ungodly. It is time she renounced all forms of image worship for the Bible commands that, "Thou shalt not make any graven image, or worship them." Exodus 20:4-5

Turn from your ways, and repent. Let the Catholic Church set aside all pride, and humble herself before the Lord God. Revisit the Scriptures and correct your errors. Take the spotlight off the Virgin Mary. Shine the light on Jesus Christ the anointed One. The one who came from eternity. The one who embodied Mary's first-born child. The one whom God named Jesus, the only begotten Son of God. The one who lived among men, and was crucified and died for the sins of mankind. The one who rose from the dead, and returned to Heaven, and is sitting at the right hand of the Father. The one Jesus Christ, whose name is the only name given among men whereby man can be saved. Salvation is through Jesus Christ only.[87] That same Jesus Christ is coming again for a church that is without spot or blemish.

To the Protestant Churches

Today Jesus is speaking to the Protestant churches. There are many faults in your midst. You are not all faithful. Calling out the Anglicans, Baptist churches, Lutherans, Reformed churches, Methodists, Seventh-day Adventists, and all Protestantism congregations. Some of you have compromised with ungodly politicians, and seek worldly recognition. Secularism is present in abundance. Many churches are lukewarm, offering no healing for the spiritually sick, and no refreshment for the spiritually weary among you. There are corrupt teachers among you who compromise with worldliness.

Some practice the doctrine of Balaam, enticing believers into sexual immorality. Some in the churches practice the doctrine of Jezebel by committing sexual immorality, and condoning sexual perversion.

Marriage is a holy institution which was ordained by God in the beginning to be between a man and a woman. Then two thousand years ago Jesus affirmed marriage as it was instituted by God in the beginning, whereby a man leaves mother and father and cleave (unites) to his wife. See Genesis 2:24, Matthew 19:5.

By defining marriage as a union between a man and a woman, Jesus dismissed all other sexual orientations, arrangements and unions as transgression of the law of God. According to God's definition of marriage, any union apart from that of a man and a woman is an unholy matrimony. Such union is not blessed by God, and is merely a nonspiritual commitment. The church of Jesus Christ should not participate in ungodly nonspiritual ceremonies.

Jesus is calling the Churches to fear God and repent and change course. The churches must call on the name of the Lord. Get back on the road that leads to Heaven. Never forget that Jesus Christ is the head of the Church. He said: "Those whom I love I reprove, and discipline, be zealous therefore and repent."[88]

To the Other Churches

A word to the Pentecostal and Nondenominational churches, and the Evangelical churches. There are also faults among you. Some of you get imbibed into filthy politics, and issues that are foreign to the Scriptures. Some preach a social gospel, and teach prosperity doctrines, and some proclaim get rich homilies. Beware of fornication among your midst. Many teachers among you deceive believers with the erroneous doctrine of once saved forever saved.

Believers who follow erroneous teachings will fall away into worldliness and commit sin, and will be spiritually lost. The prophet Ezekiel made this truth plain. He wrote that if a righteous man commit iniquity, and die in his sin, his righteousness will not be remembered.[89] The Scriptures declare that no unconfessed, and unforgiven sin will enter into the kingdom of God, and all people who die in their sins will suffer eternal punishment.

The Bible teaches that there is a heaven, and there is hell. Heaven is for the righteous ones while the ungodly is confined to hell. Shockingly, the most prominent church leader in the world; a pastor who shepherds one and a quarter billion believers, once said in an interview that there is no hell. This statement was widely reported at that time. An article in the March 29, 2018 issues of a News Magazine quoted Pope Francis saying that "There is no hell, there is disappearance of sinful souls".

The Popes statement is a complete reversal of 2,000 years of Catholic teaching, which acknowledged the existence of heaven and hell, and eternal punishment for the wicked.

Pope Francis doctrinaire statement asserts that there is no accountability for sinful deeds. Thereby implying that the souls of the wicked dead will simply vanish, and escape divine justice. Such dogmatic statement by the Catholic Pope contradicts the Bible, and runs afoul of God's divine justice.

Moreover, the perfidious statement denying the existence of hell will cause many people to live carelessly, without fear of punishment. Hell is not a myth. Hell is real. Careless believers will shipwreck their faith, and will die in their sins, and suffer everlasting torment in the Lake of Fire.

The Bible says that "The soul that sinneth, it shall die."[90] But, the soul is spirit, and spirit cannot suffer physical death. Nevertheless, the soul can suffer spiritual and eternal death. Spiritual death is the separation from God in a place of torment. The truth is that the soul also referred to as spirit belongs to God. It is God's property, and it returns to him when the person dies.[91] That soul then awaits the Day of Judgment when all men and women will give an account of their lifetime activities to God.

The souls of the righteous will go to paradise, but the souls of the ungodly and sinners will be confined to hell. However, hell is not the final home of the sinful soul. Hell is like a prison, where the accused are held until the case is tried by a judge. The confinement of an ungodly soul to hell is irreversible, and none can escape that camp of condemnation.

Hell is described as a dark place, and a place of misery, and torment and anguish. Originally, hell was made for the incarceration of millions of fallen angels, and not for man. However, the disembodied souls of sinful people will be confined there, awaiting the Day of Judgment.

Scriptures declare that after judgment, the convicted souls will be condemned to the fiery lake of burning sulfur. There they will suffer eternal punishment for their sins and evil deeds. This is the second death. The fate of the condemned souls is final, and no one will be released.[92]

Chapter 22 A Vision of Hell

Visions and dreams are not always mere series of thoughts, images, imaginations and emotions occurring during sleep. Dreams are the movements and acts of the human spirit during the time when the physical body is at complete rest during sleep. One dictionary describes dream as a supernatural experience that conveys a revelation.

Dreams and visions are therefore the means whereby the Spirit of God communicates with the spirit of man. The Scriptures affirm that God communicates with man through dreams and visions. The Lord said: "I will pour out my spirit upon all flesh; and your sons and your daughters shall prophesy, your old men shall dream dreams, and your young men shall see visions."[93]

The prophet Amos affirms that God reveals things to come to his servants.[94] God is the only one who knows the future. Scriptures tell us that God knows the end from the beginning, and tells of things yet to come.[95] Such revelations usually come through dreams. In the past, the Lord gave many dreams to people of old. Some notable ancient recipients are: Pharaoh of Egypt, Joseph, son of Jacob, King Nebuchadnezzar, the prophet Daniel, Joseph the husband of the Mary and John the revelator.

The Lord is still communicating to people today. This author has received many dreams. Some were mere wandering of the spirit while the body was in deep sleep. Yet, others were supernatural experiences,

A Vision of Hell

and revelations of places and things. I once had a vision of hell, and I still have the jitters to this day.

Of all the dreams that this author has dreamt, in his many years on Earth, none was as terrifying as the vision of hell. He recalled that he was standing at a certain unrecognized place. The day was calm and serene. There were no clouds in the sky, and the sun was shining at its brilliance. Suddenly, he realized that he had a visitor. There appeared to his right a person dressed in a long white robe. He appeared to be an angel, and he was two arm's length to my right. I could not turn my body to look at him. I was physically constrained. However, I observed him from my peripheral vision.

He started walking and I was automatically walking in step with him. We walked a few paces, and the ambiance suddenly changed. The bright light gave way to twilight, which got darker with each step. We abruptly stopped. I was now able to control my body movements. I turned and looked to my right to see the person who walked with me. To my surprise, the angel in the white robe was gone. He simply vanished.

I was now alone and standing in an eerily twilight zone. I looked around the vast area of darkness and saw nothing. Then from a very dark hole facing me, I saw two marble sized white objects dancing around in the dark. They somehow appeared to be the white of two eyes. As they moved into the twilight zone, I observed what looked like the shape of a very small man. He crouched, and was moving slowly towards me. His arms slowly swung like a windmill as he came straight at me.

The midget man appeared to be acting like a clown. He was very small in stature, and seemed to be no more than four feet tall. I kept my eyes focused on him. He approached me and swiftly reached for my arm. He missed by an inch as I pulled away just in time. He attacked again and this time he grabbed my arm. We were now engaged in a wrestling match. I fought hard and defeated him, and he backed away. He retreated in his same crouching stance; his arms in motion as he disappeared in the darkness.

I did not like the place where I found myself. I became very uneasy, and wanted to get out of the twilight zone. I turned and started walking but strangely, it appears that the entire place was moving in step with me. I was walking but made no progress. I was standing in the same spot where the man left me.

Suddenly, I saw four eyes dancing in the dark. And then four arms winding like windmills. Two midget men now advance slowly towards me. They attacked me and grabbed both arms. The battle raged and I fought as hard as I could. They were relentless in their attack, but I overcame, and they backed off and disappeared into the darkness.

I now realized the place where I was standing. The angel in the white robe took me to the gate of hell. I was shocked to find myself standing at the portals of hell. I now realized that the midget-men were devils. Apparently, their assignment was to get me into the pit of hell.

There was no way out. So far, I had two victories. I was determined that the devils will not get me into the dark place of hell. I will keep fighting, and I must keep winning. I was petrified. The devils are persistent, and they will be attacking again.

Sure enough, soon after three demons came out of the darkness. The midgets were crouching, and slowly moving towards me. Suddenly, they rushed towards me. They attacked viciously, like wild dogs. Buffeting and tormenting me. I fought hard. I punched, and kicked and screamed, but they kept charging at me. They were relentless in their attack. The three devils were too much for me. I was weakened by the continuous harassment. I could no longer fight with my hands or feet. They overpowered me, and seized both my arms and my legs. The thought of going into that dark place of hell terrified me. I felt defeated, but I would not give up.

At that point my only hope was in Jesus. But would God hear me calling from hell? I had nothing to lose, and so I decided to call for help. I kicked and wiggled as I desperately tried to free myself. In great fear, I screamed for help. I started calling on the name of Jesus. I pleaded for help, "Jesus, Jesus, help me. I don't want to go into hell."

I knew those devils were the sinful angels that rebelled against God. I began shouting to them that they will face the Judgment, and the eternal flames. I kept repeating the name of Jesus. I kept saying that

A Vision of Hell

God is going to punish the wicked devils in the Lake of Fire. When they heard those words, they backed off. However, as soon as I stopped talking, they attacked again. They rushed towards me like angry pit bulls.

The battle raged on for some time. I felt weak. Two of them grabbed my arms, and the third went behind and covered my mouth. All my strength was now gone, and I could no longer defend with the words of my mouth. I could no longer call on the name of Jesus. The devils silenced me. The devil on the right lifted my leg, and my foot off the ground. The devil on my left began to lift my other leg, while the devil behind me tightly held my mouth shut. I lost the battle. It was over. I was horrified.

Suddenly, the devil on my right let go of my right arm and my foot. The one on the left also let go of my leg and backed away. The one behind was still holding my mouth closed. When he saw that his partners backed off, he let go of my mouth and scampered away. Apparently, they saw something that scared them off and they quickly disappeared into the darkness. I thought that maybe the Lord heard my cry and chased them away.

I was very tired and weak from fighting six devils. As I stood in the dark and felt dejected, lost and without hope. Then from my peripheral vision I saw the long white robe to my side. He was the same man that left me at the entrance of hell. I was glad that he did not abandon me in hell. I was relieved by his presence. I regained the hope of getting out of that scary place of terror.

The man turned me around by his power and then started walking. To my amazement, after only a few steps I was in the brilliant light once more. The man in the white robe vanished before I could thank him, and I was alone once more. The angel in the long white robe was none other than the Lord. He took me to the gate of hell in the vision He then returned in the nick of time, and brought me out.

The Lord showed me the reality of hell so that I could testify to the world that there is a hell. There is a sobering message in that harrowing visionary experience. Let the world know that Heaven is real, and Hell is real. That demons are real and are formidable foes.

Nothing good is associated with the place called hell. The Bible paints a horrifying picture of hell. It is a place where no sane person should desire to visit. Moreover, the ticket to hell is one way. There is no return flight, and no one ever escapes from hell nor ever will.

The takeaway from this vision is that the devil is relentless in his attack against Christian believers. But the Lord Jesus is faithful. He will test you, but He will never leave you nor forsake you. The believer must trust the Lord at all times. Resist the devil and overcome temptations. He must fight the devil at all times.

The believer must remain faithful to God. He must never give up nor give in to materialism or the temporary pleasures of the world. The believer must read the Bible daily. He must pray every day, and call on the name of the Lord, and He will hear your cry and rescue you when trouble strikes. Do not give up ever. Remember this, the Lord is never late. He is always on time.

It is not the will of God that any soul should perish in hell. The Bible says that the Lord does not take pleasure in sending any soul to hell. But it is the will of God that all people come to repentance and avoid the terror of hell.[96]

People can avoid the torment of hell when they die, by accepting Jesus Christ as Lord and Savior, repenting of their sins, and turning aside from doing evil to live right. The repenting person must confess his sins to God only. Man must seek forgiveness through Jesus Christ, and not through another man, priest, saint or goddess. Jesus is the only way by which man can be saved.

Jesus Christ is the one who shed His blood, and died on the cross for the salvation of mankind. Jesus is the only way to God. Jesus is the way, the truth and the life. He is the only way to heaven. The Bible teaches that salvation is through Jesus alone, and that only God can save man from sin. Put all your faith in God, and trust not in man for your salvation.

The Apostle Peter declared that "There is no other name under heaven given among men, whereby we must be saved."[97] Do not be deceived by persuasive speakers with great sounding words, and enticing doctrines. Test all things against the word of God. It is therefore, profitable for believers to read the Bible, and know the Scriptures to avoid religious pitfalls, and recognize false teaching. Run away from the very appearance of the evil of image worship and idolatry. Shun teachings that do not give God all the adoration, and praise and honor and glory.

Christ is coming back for the Church in a little while, and many living today could well see the day of the rapture. With this in mind, Christians today should work out their own salvation, and get spiritually ready before the trumpet call of God sounds on that glorious day.

Remember this, God is worthy of all blessings and honor, and power and glory and worship; because he created all things by his will, and for his pleasure they were created.[98]

The Scriptures sum up the matter is this manner, "Man should fear God and revere and worship him, and keep his commandments, for this is the whole duty of every man, and the reason why man was created. For God will bring every deed into judgment, including every hidden thing, whether it is good or bad".[99]

Know that a day of reckoning is coming, and that all people that ever lived on Earth will face the judgment, and that man's eternal destination is either Heaven or the Lake of Fire. Therefore, it is in people's best interest to live righteously in the present state, so that on that Judgement Day, they will hear the Judge say, "well done, enter into the joys of your Lord". Whereas, the ungodly and sinners will hear the terrifying words, "Depart from me, you that do evil". It is good to seek the Lord now, before it is too late. The Scriptures declare that there is no repentance from the grave. Behold! Today is the day of salvation.

References

1. (Job 38:4-7)
2. (Isaiah 45:18)
3. (Isaiah 45:12)
4. (Ezekiel 28:18)
5. (Psalm 104:6, Genesis 1:2, 2nd Peter 3:5)
6. (Psalm 104:6-7)
7. (Genesis 8:3-8)
8. (Psalm 104:7-8)
9. (Genesis 2:7)
10. (Genesis 2:7, Zechariah 12:1, James 2:26, Ecclesiastics 12:7)
11. (Genesis 1:28)
12. (Romans 5:12)
13. (Isaiah 46:9-10
14. (Leviticus 17:11)
15. (Psalm 40:6-8)
16. (John1:29)
17. (Psalm 40:6-8, Hebrews 10:4-8) Amp. Bible
18. (Genesis 3:15)

References

19. (Deuteronomy 18:15-18)
20. (Hebrews 10:5-7)
21. (1st Corinthians 15:45)
22. (Joshua 21:11)
23. (Luke 1:56)
24. (Matthew 1:20-21)
25. (Luke 2:1-3)
26. (2 Timothy 3:16)
27. (Tacitus Annals 1:31, 2:6)
28. (Life of Augustus 27:5)
29. (Dio book 56:28)
30. (Dio book 56:28:1)
31. (Dio 56:29:2)
32. (Dio 54:34, Livius Book 138)
33. (Dio 54:35:1)
34. (Livius 138)
35. (Dio 54, Livius Book 138)
36. (Tacitus Annals 3:48)
37. (Dio 54:6, 54: 34:7). Tacitus Annals 6:10)
38. (Josephus Ant. 18:2:1)
39. (Daniel 9:25)
40. (Ezra 1:1-3)
41. (Nehemiah 2:1- 6)
42. Source: Rickard, J (19 August 2016), Artexerxes 1, (r. 464-425BC) https://www.historyofwar.org/article/people_artexerxes_1.html
43. (Daniel 9:26)
44. (Micah 5:2)
45. (Proverbs 21:1)
46. (Hebrews 10:5)

47. Retrieved online 1.9.22: https://web.uwm.edu/jewish-calendar

    Alan Corré's **Perpetual Jewish-Civil Calendar.** This **Perpetual Jewish-Civil Calendar** was created by Dr. Alan Corré (1931 – 2017), Emeritus Professor of **Hebrew** Studies at UWM

48. (2nd Samuels 7:8-17)
49. (Isaiah 7:14, 9:6-7)
50. (Luke 2: 6-7)
51. Calendar references: Credit Allan Corre - Perpetual Jewish/Civil Calendar https://web.uwm.edu/jewish-calendar/year
52. (Luke 2:10-11)
53. (Ref: Deuteronomy 18:17-19)
54. (Ref: Luke 2:14)
55. (Ref: Luke 2:17)
56. (1st Samuel 19:9-10)
57. (Matthew 8:28)
58. (John 3:16)
59. (1st Timothy 3:16)
60. (2nd Timothy 3:16).
61. (1John 4:2-3)
62. (1st Timothy 3:16)
63. (Weymouth New Testament 1904)
64. (John 3:6)
65. (Lyman Hurlbut ISBN 0-310-265-10-X)
66. (Genesis 1:1, Jeremiah 32:17)
67. (John 4:24)
68. (Luke 1:35)
69. (Amplified version: Hebrew's 10:5)
70. (Isaiah 9:6)
71. (Luke 1:35)
72. (Micah 5:2)

References

73. (John 3:34)
74. (Isaiah 9:6)
75. (Deuteronomy 6:4)
76. (John 10:30)
77. (1st Timothy 3:16 (NIV)
78. (Luke 8:10, John 16:13, 1st Corinthians 2:10)
79. (Psalm 51:5)
80. (Romans 3:23, 5:12)
81. Source: Catholic Library: Ineffabillis Deus (1854), www.newadvent.org. Retrieved 11.16.2020
82. (Matthew 13: 46-47, Mark 6:3).
83. (Will Wright, Catholic Church, History of the Church, Mary – the Blessed Mother)
84. (Luke 4:8)
85. (2nd Timothy 4:3-4)
86. (Hebrews 12:6 Amp. Version)
87. (Acts 4:12)
88. (Revelation 3:19 NAS)
89. (Ezekiel 3:20)
90. (Ezekiel 18:20)
91. (Ecclesiastes 12:7)
92. (Matthew 25:41, Revelation 21:8 NIV)
93. (Joel 2: 28)
94. (Amos 3:7)
95. (Isaiah 46:10)
96. (2 Peter 3:9)
97. (Acts 4:12)
98. (Revelation 4: 11, 7:12)
99. (Ecclesiastes 12: 13-14, Matthew 12:36)

www.ingramcontent.com/pod-product-compliance
Lightning Source LLC
LaVergne TN
LVHW051506070426
835507LV00022B/2961